DEACON BRODIE
Father to Jekyll and Hyde

Also by John S. Gibson

SHIPS OF THE '45

Deacon Brodie

Father to Jekyll and Hyde

John S. Gibson

Paul Harris Publishing

Edinburgh

First published 1977 by
Paul Harris Publishing
25 London Street
Edinburgh

© John S. Gibson 1977

Set in Monotype Baskerville

Printed in Great Britain by The Anchor Press Ltd
and bound by Wm Brendon & Son Ltd
both of Tiptree, Essex

ISBN 0 904505 24 3

Contents

Acknowledgments

When Edinburgh has laid her hand upon a man's shoulder, the memory of that touch does not readily fade.

The words are Lord Cameron's; to him my thanks for transmitting something of his deep-set feeling for old Edinburgh and the mighty traditions of Scots law.

Mr Giles Gordon first set me on the hunt for Deacon Brodie. Mrs Rosalind Mitchison and Dr William Ferguson of Edinburgh University imparted their feel for eighteenth century Scotland, as did Dr Alexander Law. Lady Mitchison gave generous advice.

Such was the richness and complexity of the city that any book about old Edinburgh is of its nature a 'combined operation'; and I am indebted to a host of friends for help in all manner of ways. They read and advised, typed, reproved, encouraged and often saw the significant details I had missed. I must also give a special word of thanks to the ladies of the Scottish Library and Edinburgh Room at the Edinburgh Public Library; to the City Museums Department, to the National Library for Scotland, to the Scottish National Portrait Gallery and to the Scottish Record Office.

J.S.G.

Illustrations

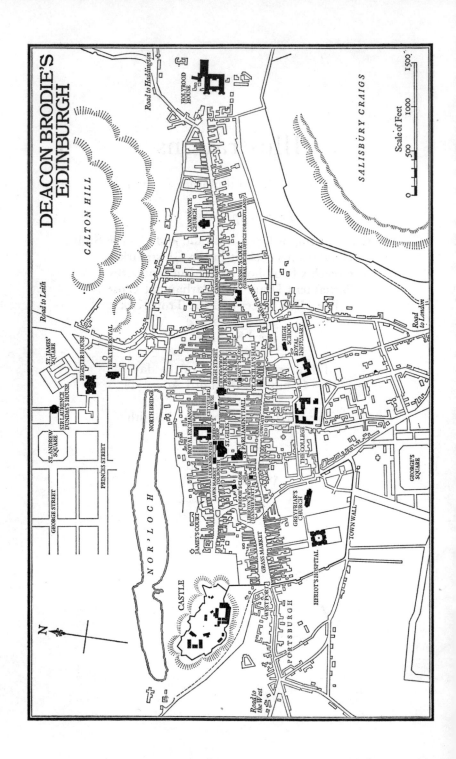

Foreword

by the Hon. Lord Cameron, D.S.C., D.L., LL.D., F.R.S.E.

The fascination of reading about crime and criminals never seems to cease; at times, however, the crimes and the criminal are of such a quality and character to warrant such an interest. In Scotland's criminal annals the activities of Edinburgh's Deacon Brodie hold a justifiable distinguished place.

The story is in truth a Tale of Two Cities: the city of respectable burgesses and professional men – Brodie's city by day; and the city of thieves, robbers, pimps and whores – Brodie's city by night, vivid, colourful and villainous. When finally detected and brought back after his flight to Holland to stand his trial for armed robbery Brodie formed the centre of a forensic drama with curious political over- and undertones which are now, for the first time, brought to light by the author of this book.

Two legendary Edinburgh figures faced each other in the High Court of Justiciary: Brodie the accused and Braxfield the Lord Justice Clerk, the presiding judge. Braxfield has suffered gravely in reputation by the criticisms of Henry Cockburn, a political adversary, whose pen was more distinguished than his judgment of a great master of the law and a fearless judge. In this trial Braxfield displayed not only his depth of legal knowledge but a patience and humanity of disposition far removed from that of the fictional Justice Clerk Weir of Hermiston of Robert Louis Stevenson's last great novel. What Mr Gibson has discovered and set down should serve in large measure to redress the balance, though Braxfield is a figure who deserves a volume to himself as a lawyer, judge and man of his century.

The defence of Brodie was in the hands of a group of Whig lawyers, chief of whom was the brilliant Henry Erskine, Dean of Faculty, and so the acknowledged leader of the Scottish Bar. It also included John Clerk of Eldin who, in this

his first memorable trial, displayed the same truculence of manner towards the Bench and extravagance of language which was to be not the least of his notable characteristics throughout a long and stormy career at the Bar. The Whig lawyers for the defence, while not neglecting the interests of their client, used the trial as a stalking horse for an exceedingly astute attack upon the Scottish 'establishment' – Tory and Dundas controlled as it was.

The crisis of the case came with the evidence of an accomplice of Brodie's whose testimony, if admitted, was fatal to the accused's chances of acquittal. As this witness was a convicted criminal, he was under Scots law 'infamous', i.e. legally incapable of giving evidence. But the prosecution conducted by Dundas law officers produced a 'King's Pardon' granted in respect of a crime committed in England which operated in accordance with English law to wipe out the pardoned transgression. Thus the pardon, it was argued, had wiped out the infamy. Maintaining this, the prosecution was on sound ground and the defence objection to the evidence of the witness was repelled. But defence counsel made as much capital as they could of such an apparent English interference with the course of Scottish justice, as Mr Gibson makes abundantly clear. Their appeal was addressed not only to the fifteen jurors in the jury box but was directed to a wider audience, the public benches, and to a nationalism which lay not far below the surface, and the inference they sought to draw was plain: that the Dundas control of Scotland was exercised not in the true interests of Scotland but in fact for their own benefit and that of their placemen and supporters. The points were not lost on the audience, whatever may have been their effect upon the jury.

One may be forgiven for pausing to devote a moment to the somewhat delightful circumstance that one of the jury who tried and convicted Brodie was no less a figure than the upright William Creech, bookseller, publisher and author, a former colleague of Brodie's on the Town Council of the city and to become Lord Provost. Creech having served on the jury, within a matter of days turned his experience to honest profit by writing, publishing and selling his account of the trial with certain admirable moral reflections upon the evil consequences of dissipation and depravity.

At the same time as presenting a masterly and vivid record of Brodie's career and trial Mr Gibson has filled in the background to the story of Brodie and his career both amorous and professional by his illuminating excursion into the daily and nightly life of the Old Town as it was in the 1780s. This double life, or at least the capacity for it, persisted long after Brodie met his fate on the Tolbooth gallows, as Mr Gibson illustrates aptly in his references to a much later *cause célèbre* of Victorian Edinburgh, the picaresque case of *Steuart v Robertson*, the tale of a 'Scotch marriage', when the stews of Clyde Street were but a literal step from the staid and austere respectability of St Andrew Square and Queen Street. After reading these pages and savouring the taste of old Edinburgh it is not difficult to divine the source from which Robert Louis Stevenson drew his Dr Jekyll and Mr Hyde. The Edinburgh of Brodie and the Edinburgh of Stevenson knew and frequented differed little in their contrasts and likenesses.

I

The Prime of William Brodie

Historic Edinburgh lay to the north and south of a valley. On the south side was the old town, the simple majestic unity of the High Street. Beneath a skyline serrated by battlement and gable, it was crowded as the underdecks of a ship of the line, every drop of water to be carried up the interminable stairs, the hearing constantly assailed by the noise of neighbours above and below, ten thousand rats in the wainscoting, many of the rooms in gloom but for a glimmer of light from some dark alley. Fire and civic improvement have put paid to most of it long since.

To the north side of the valley was, still is, the Georgian new town. Grey stone squares, streets and terraces all built by nabobs, West Indian sugar, and lawyers' fortunes. Many of them still defy the developer; but, regrettably, one square which succumbed only a few years ago was the most historic of all. For it was here, among the gaunt tenements only a bottle's throw from Princes Street, that Dr Jekyll, who by turns must be the fearful Edward Hyde, had his home. Jekyll was an Edinburgh man, the setting to the tale of horror unmistakably this decaying fringe of the Georgian town. It was a quarter of Edinburgh with particularly harrowing memories for Robert Louis Stevenson; and this was why Henry Jekyll lived there.

As a memento of the past, in a corner of what was the old square the planners have left one tenement. There it stands today, out of place as it contemplates a massive office block across the way. But, if you wish, it is still Jekyll's house; his the door with the fanlight above it in that 'square of ancient handsome houses' backing on to a disreputable little street

On misty evenings Mr Hyde still climbs its steep slope to repossess his victim.

For nearly a hundred years now 'Jekyll and Hyde' has been the currency of the English-speaking world. Everyone knows of them. Or do they? Can you separate a Scotsman from his ancestry? I think not. To understand the kindly doctor and his *alter ego* you must establish their paternity; and this leads you to another character of the town; William Brodie, Deacon of the Wrights, that is the cabinet- (and sometimes coffin-) makers of old Edinburgh.

To meet Brodie you must come deeper into the past, across the valley to the old town, to the flickering darkness of a winter's evening in the Edinburgh of 1788. The American colonies have asserted their independence. At Windsor Castle George III rules his large unhappy family. France is about to pitch herself over the cliff of revolution. But here in Edinburgh as you come out of the Parliament House between the statues of Justice and Mercy it is eight o'clock and the evening's fun is just beginning.

Above the goldsmiths' shops nestling under the old walls of St Giles, the lamps light you out of the Parliament Close into the High Street of Edinburgh. This is the *grande place* on to which scores of dark wynds debouch, abysses between the high tenements which dominate the old street on either side. On plainstanes and causeway all is noise and confusion. Highland chairmen, trotting like coolies, carry gentlemen to their drinking clubs, ladies from their tea-parties; piemen shout their wares; hefty wives hawk *'peas and beans het and warmm'*.

Beside the dark mass of St Giles, the great medieval church now divided into four kirks, the wide street is narrowed by a plain-looking tenement, CREECH in big letters above the door, the tall building known as Creech's land, Mr Creech a power in the town. Across the street is the classical order of the Royal Exchange, its banks and shops; the Town Council's first essay at the rebuilding of Edinburgh; and to their relief an investment which is now showing a profit. On the left the narrowed street runs uphill to Edinburgh Castle, where the 7th of Foot garrison the big new barracks built on the very edge of the Castle rock. On the right the *grande place* runs downhill to the

Canongate and completes its mile-long course at the Palace of Holyroodhouse. From this one splendid street the wynds and closes slant steeply away to the cesspool of the Nor' Loch on one side and to the ravine of the Cowgate on the other, like the rafters of a house-roof seen from the ridge-pole. It is the unity of the whole that makes the scene; this is the city in which Mr Pennant, the English traveller, has seen a look of magnificence 'not to be found in any other part of Great Britain'. And in the daytime from Mr Creech's windows the view over the roof tops of the Canongate leads the eye to the green hills of the eastern Lothians and the grey waters of Aberlady Bay.

It is a city that is increasing fast in numbers. Twenty years ago the ancient city walls held most of its sixty thousand. Now the numbers are nearly half as much again, and the great *lands*, some of them twelve storeys high, their common stairs as filthy as they are steep and dark, are grossly overcrowded. Where, it is being asked, will everyone get a Christian burial? Already the congestion in the kirkyard of the Greyfriars is causing concern; and the general view is that only the coldness of the climate and the acidity of the smoke from the town's ten thousand chimneys has prevented it becoming a breeding ground of pestilence.

In the flickering half-darkness the guide at your side, one of the select corps of the town's cadies on duty all day long and far into every night, reels off in his Highland sing-song the names of the gloomy entries into the great tenements fronting the street: Writer's Court and the Advocate's Close. The Anchor Close, the Fishmarket Close and the Fleshmarket Close. The Assembly Close where the City Guard is now headquartered – a ferocious-seeming body of men in old red uniforms and cocked hats. Bell's Wynd and Borthwick's Wynd. Halkerston's Wynd where a Laird of Halkerston died sword in hand when an English army burned the city; now it is a place of ill repute.

You pass the old Burgh Cross. When the hands of the clock on the tower of St Giles are at noon the same gentlemen whom you see around you on their way to club and tavern will meet here to collect moneys and exchange gossip. Now it is eight o'clock and near the Cross the Gillespie brothers have closed their snuff-shop and Messrs Inglis and Horner are also putting up their shutters; the ladies of Edinburgh are done with their

buying of silks for the day. The cadie leads you on through the hubbub on the street, past the Covenant Close which runs down to the Cowgate, past the great Tron Kirk and its Dutch steeple, past houses now encroaching on the street in the uncertain lamplight, with timber galleries curiously carved. It is still the city of King James VI.

But if it is still historic Edinburgh, the city is now discarding its Scots identity as summarily as the servant lassies dispose of their slops. A year past was taken down the ancient house where Mary Stewart looked through prison bars on the mob shouting 'Burn the whure!' The integrity of the *grande place* has now been breached so that great bridges may span the valley to the north and the Cowgate ravine to the south. No more does cosy Edinburgh hold that Wood's Farm would be too windy ever to be habitable. The New Town is under way; and it is all the rage to live in one of the plain-looking terraces speculative builders are throwing up in these quail-haunted fields. Venerable gentlemen and their ladies may still keep to the old town, but fashion, learning and the law are on the move. Harry Erskine, the son of an earl and the brightest star of Parliament House, was born in a venerable building at the head of Gray's Close off the High Street: his address is now a smart new house at Number 53 Princes Street. A teacher of French scratches a living in the house where a judge lived in some style twenty years past. In another a rouping wife keeps a salesroom for old furniture. The old town is dying, but does not yet know it.

Also on the way to abandonment is the old Scots tongue. Jostling in the street, city dignitary and city lamplighter abuse each other in much the same language. Lord Braxfield, the Lord Justice Clerk, talks of the 'hingin o' scoondrels'; and when the Cape Club meets in the Isle of Man Tavern the Scots is as broad as the fun. Reading the decorous English of the *Edinburgh Evening Courant* you'd never guess it was so. Polite Edinburgh is anglicizing its speech. 'The ladies of Edinburgh', a young traveller from London has noted, 'talk very grammatically, are peculiarly attentive to the conformity of their words to their ideas, and are great critics in the English tongue.' So are the young advocates of Parliament House. As they say, David Hume the atheist died confessing not his sins but his scotticisms.

To shine in literature is to write good English. Some twelve years past there died a crack-brained lawyer's clerk who tried his hand at the Scotch vernacular. His theme was neither country churchyards nor the vanity of human wishes but the daily life of the town. The sun as it comes up over the horizon beyond the Bass Rock lighting the old crown of St Giles; the mighty noise in the drinking clubs. The grumbling of the causeway at the weight of waggon wheels; the joy of the plainstanes at a pretty girl's foot. Edinburgh in the summer going to amuse itself on the sands at Leith; Edinburgh on a drenching winter's day, 'when big as burns the gutters rin' and there is company and a dram of gin in Luckie Middlemist's. Young Robert Fergusson's cronies liked his verse, but the critics took no serious notice. They have been taking more notice of Mr Burns from Ayrshire, but are far from sure about the wisdom of his resorting to the language of the common people.

Handsome, energetic Edinburgh, her confusion of identity goes beyond her speech. She is the capital of Scotland but the Stewart dynasty is all but ended; two months past Prince Charles Edward was buried in Rome and with him all Jacobite hopes. The Palace of Holyroodhouse lies neglected, its State Gallery dirty as a stable, the tapestries all faded, the fine ceilings hanging down. The noblest prospect to the clever and calculating is the high road south of Berwick, but Fergusson here caught the instinctive feelings of the people. Black be the day that ever our forefathers put Scotland under the English yoke. To Hell with the Union.

Religion too can be a source of confusion. It is not so much that this is the city of David Hume as well as of John Knox, and that from his house over in St Andrew Square *le bon David* radiated scepticism. In this, not many of his fellow townsmen paid any attention to him; he was just another eccentric like Lord Monboddo, who thought that children were born with tails. It is not that there is any confusion in the message from the pulpits. The Edinburgh ministers speak earnestly and at length to the people every Sunday morning, and then again every Sunday afternoon. Even the poor put on their best clothes for kirk on Sunday. There must be good in all this.

And yet, though the ministers command attention, as Mr Edward Topham, a traveller from the south, has written in

Anglican disapproval, the nonsense sometimes heard from the pulpits is wellnigh incredible. As for the congregation, though the people droving into the kirks look as sorrowful as if they were going to bury themselves as well as their sins, and the sabbath casts a spell on everyone, 'at other times – and even on Sundays out of the public gaze – there is no crime they would scruple to commit'. The parade of goodness lends itself to hypocrisy and deceit. Even in the most calvinist of households there is some confusion, but here it is rather a genuine doubt about the smaller pleasures of life. 'Bairns, it is *too* guid', Mr Scott, W.S., is disposed to say to his boys at George's Square should young Walter, his son, exclaim at the goodness of the broth simmering in its tureen; as he speaks he pours a jugful of cold water on to the soup.

Fortunately, religion does not depress the ladies: they are the flowers of Edinburgh. 'Love reconciles me to a Scotch accent which from the mouth of a pretty woman is simply and sweetly melodious', James Boswell has written as he installed his mistress in a house in Borthwick's Close. Mr Topham would agree with him. 'Their hearts are soft and full of passion' is his verdict, and in the two winters he spent in Edinburgh he was quick to learn. All too soon they lose their looks, he says. 'After a particular time they grow large and lusty, which gives their features and shape a coarse and masculine appearance', but the younger women have 'a certain proportion of *embonpoint* and voluptuousness which makes them highly the objects of luxurious love'. 'Handsome, light-haired, fair complexions with freckles', another traveller from the south has noted, adding in an ecstasy of recollection 'along the streets they have a noble walk'. Continuing in his enthusiastic vain, perhaps not altogether to be believed, and certainly to some hoots of derision from the citizens when they read his book, Topham (of Eton and Trinity College, Cambridge) has praised their sociability, their affability, modesty and politeness; their fondness of admiration and flattery – and pleasure. What swept him off his feet was a visit to an Oyster Cellar party.

Here, one evening, in a cavern of a room off a dark close he found a large and brilliant company of both sexes seated round a big table. It was covered with dishes of oysters and pots of porter. Tallow candles cast a dim light over the scene. Brandy punch followed the porter and the fun began.

The women, who, to do them justice, are much more entertaining than their neighbours in England, discovered a great deal of vivacity and fondness for repartee. A thousand things were hazarded and met with applause, to which the oddity of the scene gave propriety, and which could have been produced in no other place. When the company were tired of conversation, they began to dance reels, their favourite dance, which they performed with agility and perseverance.

Alas, the menfolk were not quite up to it. The evening was brought to an end too soon in the middle of a reel. 'One of the gentlemen fell down in the most active part of it, and lamed himself.' The ladies now found it was time to retire and called for their sedans 'and away they went, and with them all our mirth'.

The Scots girl indeed is more than a snowy bosom. She is educated, can talk with wit and verve, and has a freedom of style a whole world away from covenanting times or indeed her English sister. The gentlemen have proposed that the Pantheon Debating Club should be for men only; to this the spokeswoman for the ladies has replied in faultless verse: if you deny us access, she has said, that is a game that two can play!

> The Eastern prophet did exclude,
> All women from his heaven,
> And in our time a dread command,
> By Pantheonites is given.

> That now no fair shall entrance find,
> In to the learned hall,
> As Salique law precludes the sex,
> From ruling over Gaul.

> But gods beware, perhaps ere long,
> You sorely will repent,
> We can deny you access too,
> 'Tis time then to relent.

Handsome, intellectual Edinburgh, a place of 'pleasure, rapture and delight', where everything has still a certain homeliness of style. When the kirk elders meet between sermons on Sundays to stretch their legs, first they study the wind. Should it blow from the west they take their walk along half-finished Princes Street to the village of Dean; if from the east they saunter down the Canongate to the King's Park and

Salisbury Craigs; and so the smoke of Auld Reekie is avoided. Jamie Laing, the depute Town Clerk, holds that the Highlanders of the City Guard should not be idle in the summer months when nights are short and blackguarding at a minimum; so in the long evenings he parades them on the Meadows and they dig up moles. And all day long, as you come in from the High Street to buy your silks, the big key of Messrs Inglis and Horner's shop hangs on a nail by the door.

'*Fear God in Luve*', '*Oh Lord in thee is all my traist*', '*Be pasient in the Lord*', say the legends above the dark closes, voices from a bygone age, as you go down the Canongate. Here the buildings are still lofty, the blue-bonneted cadie still needed to help you find your way. If it is your will, he will find you a lady of pleasure. (If so it would be wise to be guided by him; to catch the clap, they say, is to get a pair of Canongate breeches.) But on learning that it is the big new buildings in Chessel's Court you are seeking he will recognize that this is not your purpose, though he will wonder all the more what you are up to at this time of night.

Here in Chessel's Court, by the flicker of the oil lamps, you are to watch a small drama. Dimly you see a large house built of grey stone in the decent Scots style. In front is a railed courtyard, in the shadows of which lurks a man with a slouch hat and a grey coat. In from the Canongate comes a servant girl. The sixth sense of the Edinburgh lass out after dark detects the stranger in the shadows, and she hurries on her way. Then there is the sound of quick footsteps, and into the courtyard scurries the well-known figure of Mr James Bonar, a small legal gentleman come back from the dinner-table to pick up some papers from his office before it closes for the night. He goes up to try the house's front door. As he makes to enter, a man, black coat, black cocked hat, erupts from the passageway within and runs off into the darkness.

The grey-coated watcher in the shadows sees this, and, as the little gentleman goes inside, is doubly anxious. When Mr Bonar re-emerges from the doorway and scurries off as he came, the watcher blows three blasts on an ivory pocket-whistle, the sound thin and shrill, and himself runs away. To complete the sequence, two figures then come furtively out of the doorway and go off into the night.

It has the appearance of a bungled breaking and entering.

So it is; but Mr Bonar is Deputy Solicitor of the Excise; this the General Excise Office housing the revenues of Scotland; and the misfired crime the culmination to a long series which has shocked the city. There is even more to it than this. One of the miscreants is William Brodie, Deacon of the Wrights, a powerful figure on the Town Council, a big man in the town. When it comes out the scandal will be in keeping.

A wright is Scots for cabinet-maker, the word being pronounced *wiricht* with a firm burl to the 'r': the Deacon of the Wrights was the head of his craft. In this year of grace, 1788, Deacon Brodie was forty-seven but looked much younger; from cocked hat to silver shoe buckles, he was rather a dandy. Out of a sallow face shone his big brown eyes, one of them with a slight cast which, people thought, gave him the look of a Jew. A nasty scar showed livid on one cheek. He also had an odd style of walking: long strides, knees slightly bent, and at each step a way of striking the plainstanes of the High Street with his heel. In all he did, in the way he looked, in the way he spoke, there was something of the mystery man.

Brodie was the name of ancient landed family in the north-east of Scotland. In the corn lands and woodlands round Forres there had been Brodies since the time of Macbeth. Brodie of Brodie held (indeed, holds) Brodie Castle, and the Brodie gentry had spread over the Laigh of Moray and into the rough hill land that leads over to the Spay. Sometime in the late seventeenth century the son of the Brodie Laird of Milntown came to Edinburgh to learn the law and be the family's man of business, making their wills, borrowing money for them, and seeing to disputes in the Court of Session they might have with the neighbouring Grants, Ogilvies, or Roses. This Brodie sprig did well, and when he died he was the capital's oldest Writer to the Signet as well as a centenarian. By then Francis, his son, was well up in years and prospering as a *wiricht*. In this Edinburgh where gentry and burgesses alike were filling their houses off the dark wynds with cabinets and chests of drawers, wardrobes and wine-coolers, chairs for the parlour, tables for dining, Francis Brodie could not but do well; under the guidance of William Adam the architect, he had already made his name with an elegant refurnishing of the

Duke of Hamilton's apartments at Holyroodhouse. A judicious marriage crowned his success. In 1740 he espoused the daughter of another Edinburgh lawyer who had come from the north-east. For the purposes of 'makin muckle mair', still more important than her landed connections was the fact that this union made him son-in-law to a member of the Merchant Guild. By this door he too entered their select society.

In Horse Wynd, off the foot of the Canongate, a big new tenement was now Brodie property; so was another in World's End Close and one near Parliament House. Approached from the Lawnmarket by a wynd – already known as Brodie's Close – was the family's spacious home, its ceilings high, its windows to the west big and arched. A distinguished burgess of the time of King James the Sixth had built it; and it was one of the best houses in the town. Here Cicel Brodie bore her husband eleven children. But the family Bible makes melancholy reading: seven died in infancy and were buried among the weeds and thistles of the kirkyard of Greyfriars. Four survived; William their first born; Francis, his younger brother by eight years; and Jean and Jacobina, two much younger sisters.

In this comfortable Edinburgh, his father become a rich man, his uncle a well-known surgeon at the new Royal Infirmary the Town Council had recently built, young William had his schooling with the sons of other burgesses in the ramshackle building above the Cowgate which had served the town as High School since the days of King James the Sixth. It is not easy to put yourself into the shoes of an eighteenth-century schoolboy, least of all the square-toed, so shapeless as to fit either foot, shoes of a pupil of the High School of Edinburgh. In his memoirs Henry Cockburn was to damn the eighteenth-century school so effectively that the mind's eye sees too readily the snivelling youngsters at their desks, the torture of *Wedderburn's Rudiments of Latin Grammar*, the daily flogging. For the High School which young Brodie knew, a much smaller place, its roll still under the two hundred mark, a surer guide are the memories of his schoolmate Henry Mackenzie, doyen of Mr Creech's *literati*. To Mackenzie, one master was 'a great favourite of his pupils'; another 'a good-humoured man with a great deal of comedy about him, also liked by his class'; a third was easy-going to a fault: only one 'a frequent flogger'. The diet of Latin grammar of which Cockburn complained was only for beginners. Sometimes the boys had a panoramic glimpse of old Rome in the ordained progression through Virgil, Horace, Sallust, Cicero and Livy; some of the brilliance of the masters rubbed off on the boys. The hours were severe rather than savage. There was indeed a seven o'clock start, but by nine the boys had dispersed to their homes for breakfast. Back at ten they broke at noon for three hours, dinner still being the event of the early afternoon, this in turn followed by a final two hours of instruction. This was not a schooling to suppress a lively boy.

There were also extra-curricular influences such as a prissy youngster like Cockburn would not know. The taverns of the Cowgate were open to young and old alike, some of them none too reputable. Even a couple of decades later, in the school intervals young Walter Scott would foregather with his cronies round Lucky Brown's fireside. His purpose, he said, was to exercise on an audience of his peers his genius as a raconteur. In their day others – young Brodie perhaps – would put their introduction to tavern life to different uses, and as Mr Creech was to observe, were 'soon initiated in folly and vice'.

We do not know what at this stage of his life young Brodie felt about Edinburgh and its ways; or of the implacable God of his fathers and His responsibility for the gravestones of so many infant Brodies in the kirkyard of the Greyfriars. What we do know about him is that he had no wish to succeed his father as Edinburgh's foremost cabinet-maker. As he was to recall the day before he died, at this stage he wanted to go to sea. It was the year which saw the opening shots of the Seven Years War. Before he was much older, week in, week out, the *Courant* and the *Caledonian Mercury* carried intelligence of handsome windfalls for lucky lieutenants (fortunes for their admirals) from prizes taken at sea. Nearer home, Thurot the Frenchman from Dunkirk had the Leith merchants in alarm, his frigates lurking off the mouth of the Forth. And in 1759, the year of Quebec and Quiberon Bay, it would be particularly hard for an imaginative youngster to reconcile himself to a carpenter's bench. But in this he had to reckon with his father.

By now Francis Brodie had won himself a place of importance in the running of the town. His fellow builders, carpenters and cabinet-makers had elected him their Deacon, or leader;

and as Deacon of the Wrights he was head of far and away
the biggest of the incorporated trades of Edinburgh, respon-
sible for the training, conduct and welfare of its members. He
also served on the Town Council; and this brought its own
blessings. By a custom which was to outlast the old town,
members of the Council enjoyed the monopoly of the public
work which collectively they sanctioned. Thus, were the door
of the Old Tolbooth to be beaten in by a rioting mob, were
there to be a new shop door fitted with the repaving of the
streets, did the galleries of the Tron Church need repair, were
there an improved town gallows to be erected, it was the Deacon of the Wrights who benefited.

Councillors did more than feather their nests. From the
dingy Council chamber next to St Giles, still more from
Cleriheugh's tavern to which they would adjourn to wet their
whistles, they ran the town. They maintained the preserves of
all the city trades and crafts: the surgeons and goldsmiths; the
tailors, cordiners and hammermen; the barbers and candle-
makers, weavers and waulkers. They enforced monopolies big
and small, from the privilege of printing newspapers to the
monopoly of hiring chaises to the port of Leith. The port of
Leith itself they ruled, and the fisheries of the Forth, the best
oyster beds in Europe. A seat in Parliament at far-off Westminster, professorships at the University, teaching posts at the
High School off the Cowgate, the filling of the city's pulpits,
captaincies in the Town Guard, the town's entire officialdom,
all were in their gift. They elected themselves and were
steadfast for the King's interest and the existing order of things.
'Omnipotent, corrupt, impenetrable', Henry Cockburn was
to call them, perhaps a little too shrilly; 'silent, submissive,
mysterious and irresponsible'. Their grip of the town was
absolute. For all the hold the town's people had over them,
as Cockburn was to say, they might have been sitting in Venice.

Though to be in trade was to have a mere middle place in
the Edinburgh pecking order in which advocates took prece-
dence over Writers to the Signet, the W.S. over the surgeon,
and in which the established trades were uppish about milliners
and room-setters, to be a town councillor was to have power.
It would not have been difficult for Francis Brodie to prevail
on the Member of Parliament for the city, dependent as he
was on the Town Council's votes, to find a midshipman's berth

for his restless son; or to bring the necessary pressure on the Secretary to the Admiralty through his landed connections in the north-east. They too would know members of parliament who could have their arms twisted. It is a fair assumption that the thought of doing so never entered old Francis's mind. William was to go into the family business, and that was an end of it.

Still unmarried as he progressed through his twenties and thirties, William Brodie might well have become no more than yet another card in the Edinburgh pack. It was the coming of theatre to Edinburgh that changed him. A generation before there had been a playhouse in a wynd off the Canongate. The ministers of religion, the mob, and the likes of old Francis had soon seen to its closure. But now the green slope of Multersey's Hill at the far end of the half-built North Bridge had been 'appropriated to Satan'. By Edinburgh initiative a theatre in the style of a playhouse in one of the smaller European capitals had been raised and a London actor-manager with a company of players imported. The exhilaration was profound. 'Edinburgh', wrote young Topham, 'which has been for a long time without trade or company, a mere mass without spirits, seems to be animated with new life.'

The Theatre Royal, as it called itself, was an immediate success. In pit, stalls and galleries the audience listened attentively to English as it should be spoken, as were enacted before their eyes *The Nabob*, *The Bankrupt*, *Piety in Pattens*, some Shakespeare, and *The Beggar's Opera*. Everyone was delighted; even the poor in the gods forebore to pelt the stage with apple runts and half-eaten oranges as was the way at Drury Lane. But of all the pieces in the company's limited repertoire none was more popular than *The Beggar's Opera*; and none had a more electric effect on William Brodie.

Reading today the sprightly libretto of John Gay's masterpiece, and thinking oneself back to, say, an Edinburgh winter's night of two hundred years ago, one can see why. To be carried in a sedan from the big house in Brodie's Close, through the clamour of the High Street, down the steep darkness of Halkerston's Wynd, then up the hill to the new Shakespeare Square, through the doric pillars of the little theatre into the crowded and candlelit auditorium, this would be a kind of wonder. And when the actors came on, and Peachum was quickly into

> 'Tis woman that seduces all mankind,
> By her we first were taught the wheedling arts,
> Her very eyes can cheat; when she's most kind,
> She tricks us of our money with our hearts.

it was magic unalloyed.

Everyone loved the songs. On a jaunt to London one winter night in 1774 James Boswell and a travelling companion passed a tedious stage in the coach journey through County Durham by singing them one after the other. At the Theatre Royal Macheath the dashing highwayman was invariably played by West Digges, an erstwhile army officer, often short of money but never of charm, the beau ideal of Edinburgh society. For William Brodie it seems *The Beggar's Opera* had a deeper meaning. Others might limit themselves to the pleasing possibility of Polly Peachum, a slave on Indian soil, mocking the sultry toil, reposing on their breast. Macheath himself wanted only a sufficiency of ladies at all times. To Brodie the play suggested a plan for living. To him its topsy-turvy world, every value reversed, every man with his price (every woman too), where prisons were for escaping from, and the whole of life was suffused with excitement, this stood in marked contrast to humdrum Edinburgh where you were too much known and too little appreciated. The play's message of anarchy, as if someone today were to stage a musical about the Kray twins, thrilled him to the core. Beyond women and wine, is there aught else, sang Jemmy Twitcher and his criminal friends. To Brodie there was indeed something better in life than this – to hoodwink the whole town and outsmart authority. And he would have ample opportunity to refresh himself with the new wisdom. West Digges's company was small and underpaid; its repertoire sadly limited. In these years of the early seventies *The Beggar's Opera* was played again and again. Whenever it was performed William Brodie would be in his box.

That is, if he was not at the nightly meetings of the Cape Club which provided the other means of escape from the grey reality of Edinburgh. The Cape was not the meeting place of the professors and lawyers with literary pretensions who crowded Creech's bookshop in the morning. Unlike the Wig Club, whose staple was indecency, its very ballot box a grotesque wooden torso offensive to delicate sensibilities, the Cape's membership was not the landed gentry. It was not quite so given over to bawdy song as the Crochallan, for which poet Burns was to compose some of his ripest pieces; nor was it as nationalist as the Poker, which stirred the embers of resentment at Westminster's distrust of things Scottish. What marked out the Cape from its score of contemporaries, crammed nightly into taverns and drinking dens, was its bright streak of fantasy. A burlesque of masonic rights initiated the new member, and a red velvet cap sat on its President's wig. Business was conducted with a nonsense ritual, members were known to each other by comic names, each in allusion to some scrape or misadventure. The membership was the cards of old Edinburgh; these, the painters and the players from the Theatre Royal.

Fergusson, the wild young poet who in his verse caught the spirit of the Cape and so much else of the town, had led the singing and been Sir Precentor. Alexander Runciman the painter was a member; so was Henry Raeburn, Sir Discovery to the Cape long before King George knighted him. At Cape suppers (London porter, welsh rabbits, and Loch Fyne herring), David Herd sang the Scots songs he collected. James Watt who made steam engines work was sometimes there; so was Rennie the bridge builder. Brodie's Cape-name was Sir Lluyd, the point coming clear as you pronounce it, and when you read that two of his cronies were Sir Roger and Sir Stark Naked.

While old Francis still presided over his family in the big house down Brodie's Close, his elder son turned an acceptable face to the world. He was now Edinburgh's chief cabinet-maker in the golden age of that craft; his the leading role in this particular blossoming of the art of living. When the old man was struck by a paralysing illness from which recovery was not to be expected William succeeded him as Deacon of the Wrights, and with this had the early prospect of a seat on the Town Council. Now, in middle life, William had his chance to make his mark. Now Edinburgh would be unable to ignore him any longer.

The year was 1781, and it happened that William was joining the Council at a bizarre moment in the history of that exclusive body. The Council had contrived to return two rival members of Parliament to Westminster, and the town, as they said in those days, was in a *turrivee*. For nearly twenty years Sir Laurence Dundas had been the member for Edinburgh. He was of a different batch of Dundases from the Midlothian family of that name which gripped power and patronage so firmly in its hands in those decades; but this disability was balanced by his great wealth. Not for nothing had he been Commissary-General to the Army. Since 1762 he had enjoyed the reward of a baronetcy, good going for an Edinburgh bailie's son who had served behind a shop counter in his youth. But now that he was advancing in years Sir Laurence was getting above himself: he wanted a peerage.

King George would not agree, no matter how long the ancestry of Dundas bonnet-lairds behind the Edinburgh bailie, Sir Laurence's father. Perhaps great Henry of the Midlothian Dundases, he who was the member for the county and becoming so important as Mr Pitt's right hand at distant Westminster, was unsympathetic too. Sir Laurence was furious and took the opportunity of the famous Commons resolution that the power of the Crown 'had increased, was increasing and ought to be diminished' to cross the floor of the House and vote with the King's unfriends. Loyal Edinburgh was shocked and, with Sir Laurence up for re-election in 1780, resolved to act. To many of the Town Council, like old Francis, it was unforgivable that their member of Parliament should so desert the sovereign when the rebellion in America was going badly for the King's army; anyhow, they had known his father, and in Scotland that is generally a good reason for cutting a public figure down to size. And so they elected a young and promising advocate as Member for Edinburgh. Sir Laurence's following, led by the Lord Provost, gathered round him. The Town Council split in two, each faction claiming the right to appoint the new member. For close on a year there was deadlock; and it was in the middle of this that old Francis withdrew to his rocking-chair, and his son took over from him.

To the two factions, William Brodie soon made it clear that he was open to offers, and with the rival factions so evenly balanced, all eyes were on the new Deacon. The two halves of the Town Council importuned. William Brodie hummed and hawed. All along he had been something of a mystery to his contemporaries. Now people wondered what he was up to. Did he want a sweetener? The general view was that this was it, and that it all had to do with the baronet's fine new house. By greasing the Town Clerk's palm a few years past Sir Laurence had got a feu of the plum site in St Andrew Square (it had been meant for a church). Here he had had one of the best classical architects of the day build a mansion for him. It was a little miracle of taste – and it still stands today as if it had strayed from Italy or the Faubourg St Germain into the New Town of Edinburgh. Its rooms were the last word in elegance, but Sir Laurence had been so unwise as to fill them with furniture by the London cabinet-makers. Was it that Deacon Brodie felt that he was every bit as good as craftsman as Mr Chippendale?

An anecdote of Henry Mackenzie's in his old age conveys the puzzled amusement the town took at the spectacle of the new Deacon of the Wrights squeezing Sir Laurence Money-bags. Late one evening Ross of Pitcalnie, a Highland laird, the tenant of the top flat in the Brodie mansion and something of a wag, was being carried through St Andrew Square in a sedan chair. Mischievous with drink he called at Sir Laurence's new house and announced himself as Deacon Brodie. Up went a footman to the baronet's bedroom, Sir Laurence being confined there with an attack of gout; down he came with a message that the Deacon was to make himself comfortable, accept a bottle of champagne and a midnight supper while his host rose from his bed. The denouement, when the gouty baronet hobbled downstairs to find that he had been duped was a fine Edinburgh joke for a while.

Obligingly, Sir Laurence died later that year, and so the dispute as to who should be the member for Edinburgh came to an end. But the question remained, what had been the Deacon's game?

The town went on wondering as William Brodie strengthened his position on the Council. Deacon of the Wrights in 1782 and 1783 as well as in 1781; Trades Councillor in 1784; Deacon of the Wrights again in 1786 and 1787; all this carrying with it a seat on the Town Council. As was the prerogative of the post, he did well out of contracts for burgh work. The Council had resolved to clear away the ancient cobbles of the High Street and lower its level. Up and down the *grande place* there was work for the Deacon of the Wrights in fitting new doors (and locks) to shops. As the grey streets edged westward he was speculating in the building of the New Town, and the new housing also gave his cabinet-maker's business splendid opportunities. Still in middle life, the Deacon might well go further. Why not Lord Provost of the Royal Burgh of Edinburgh some day? Then, perhaps, a knighthood from King George at Windsor? It had happened to others. It could happen to him.

However, by the middle of the decade a strange story was current in Edinburgh. Deacon Brodie, it was said, had sprung a convicted criminal from the Tolbooth, that tall, gaunt building abutting on the west side of St Giles which in its day had served as Town Council Chamber, thieves' hole, meeting place of the old Scots Parliament, incarceration for Covenanters as they waited to have their thumbs crushed under questioning, and as the town gaol. The escapee was the son of a Grassmarket stabler named Hay and he was due a hanging for a murder he had undubitably committed.

The escape was ordinary enough, the means being a visit by the lad's father the night before the execution was to take place and a plentiful supply of drink to make the gaoler tipsy. But in the story which went flying round the town the Brodie touch showed in the use made of Edinburgh superstition. The stabler's son had to be hidden until means could be found to get him out of the country, so he had been concealed in the one hiding place in the town where no one would dare look. Sir George Mackenzie, 'Bluidy Mackenzie', had been the tormentor of the Covenanters a hundred years past. Naturally his big pretentious tomb in the kirkyard of the Greyfriars was both haunted by his ghost and shunned by the townsfolk. Under its cupola Brodie had his escapee lodged; and since young Hay had been schooled at the neighbouring Heriot's Hospital some Heriot's schoolboys duly sworn to secrecy were recruited to keep him in victuals in his lair. The stabler's son had had a lucky escape. Just as fortunate had been the Deacon's reputation. Although the story – too good to be kept hidden – soon reached Mr Creech's ears at his bookshop in the Lawnmarket, nothing could be pinned on his fellow councillor, the Deacon of the Wrights.

But now he was also putting his reputation at risk by keeping two mistresses, and two families of infant Brodies from the wrong side of the blanket. Mistress Anne Grant of Cant's

Close had twice made old Francis a grandfather before he died. There was nothing unusual in this. James Boswell had kept a mistress in a cosy house down Borthwick's Close under the nose of his severe old father. By-blows were common as gambling debts. The coming judge Lord Braxfield had fathered one, and no one thought much the worse of him for that. But now there was also Mistress Jeannie Watt of Libberton's Wynd; Lucy Lockit as well as Polly Peachum. William Brodie's mother had been a Grant; from what we know of her, Mistress Grant may have been a respectable domestic from Aberdeen-shire or the Laigh of Moray who had fallen to Francis's elder son. Jeannie Watt was a lady of the town.

Then there was his infatuation with the excitement and the bloodletting at the cockpit which his friend Michael Henderson had built behind his stables in the Grassmarket. There was nothing uncommon in this either; peers as well as ruffians and town councillors made up Henderson's clientele at matches between, say, the cocks of Lanark and those of Haddington-shire. Betting was heavy and big money changed hands, except that, as Mr Topham observed, shortage of ready cash some-times made settlement difficult.

Meanwhile, the bachelor Deacon lived in some style in the house down Brodie's Close. Over in the New Town, his favourite sister Mistress Jamie, married to a well-doing upholsterer, was esconced in a big new tenement in St James's Square. Her younger sister, Mistress Jean, kept house for him. Was she disturbed by the presence of Mistress Watt and her involuntary nephews only a pistol-shot away in Libberton's Wynd, by the gamecocks clucking away in their cages in the yard, by her brother forever bursting into snatches from *The Beggar's Opera*? Perhaps not; and clearly she suspected nothing sinister from the house-breakings, shop-breakings and other villainies which suddenly afflicted the town.

These began in the August of 1786. One night a counterfeit key opened the door of Messrs Johnston and Smith, bankers in the Royal Exchange, and £800 sterling disappeared from the drawers. Most of the banknotes were of the reigning triumvirate, the Bank of Scotland, the Royal Bank and the British Linen; and the *Edinburgh Evening Courant* told its readers that Messrs

Johnston and Smith offered any informer a reward of five for every hundred recovered.*

This bait took no fish, but two days after the robbery, a parcel wrapped in grey paper was left at the door of the Town Council Chambers, the dingy building on the west side of St Giles. It held a third share of the loot: £250 of the missing banknotes. At the Sheriff-Clerk's office Mr William Scott, Procurator-Fiscal† for the shire of Edinburgh, must have been as puzzled by the return of the money as by the robbery itself.

On the night of the 9th of October Mr James Wemyss, goldsmith in the Parliament Close, had the misfortune of having his shop broken into, and was consequently the poorer by half a hundred gold and diamond rings, brooches and ear-rings galore. He also lost a miscellany of spoons; table-spoons and teaspoons, tureen spoons, and punch spoons, all silver. Reporting the crime, the *Courant* said that information should be passed either to Mr Scott or to the Deacon – that is the President – of the Incorporation of Goldsmiths of Edin-burgh. But the reward proffered was a mere ten guineas.

This again was not enough; the crimes went on. December came, the month in which literary gentlemen turned their gaze on the phenomenon of a ploughman-poet new come from Ayr-shire, so bold as to want published an Edinburgh edition of his verse; and from his lodgings in Libberton's Wynd Robert Burns wrote in wonder: 'You may expect to see my birthday inserted among the wonderful events in the Poor Robin's and Aberdeen Almanacks, along with the Black Monday and the Battle of Bothwell Bridge. My Lord Glencairn and the Dean of Faculty, Mr H. Erskine have taken me under their wing.'

The shopkeepers of Edinburgh would be more taken up with their own troubles. The building of the great bridges and their broad streets spanning the valleys to north and south had brought in its train the opening of a vast number of new shops. Now McKain's the hardware merchants of Bridge Street had had a nocturnal visitor. Nothing had been stolen, but he had been there; the lock which should have kept him out had been opened. Then a week before Hogmanay, from their neighbours the Messrs Bruce's new shop at the corner of Bridge Street and

---

* For this and all succeeding references to money, multiply by twelve to reach present-day (1977) values.

† *Anglice* crown prosecutor.

the High Street, watches and jewellery vanished in the night time; it was the more galling for Mr John and Mr Andrew Bruce that they had just had a new shop door and lock fitted. That Christmas Day there was to be a double blow. While the town was recovering from the traditional roasted goose, Mr Tapp of the Parliament Close had his goldsmith's shop broken into. Now the city was in great alarm. Up to now the common night-time disturbance had been the sound of breaking glass as parties in taverns wound up a good evening, and that was nobody's business but their own. House- and shopbreaking had been unknown; the cadies had seen to that. The fearsome faces of the City Guard, exercising in the High Street by day, at sentinel posts throughout the town by night, might be no deterrent to the artful thief. But the cadies too were on call at all hours at their stance near St Giles. They knew every stranger and his business the moment he arrived in town. They kept the Sheriff-Clerk's men informed of what the various bad hats were up to. How terrifying then that in this crowded city where the tall lands and the dark wynds gave vice both its chance and the possibility of concealment criminals should now be on the loose!

Or was it a matter of thieves and rogues? There were disturbing stories of a masked figure moving as if by magic through the locked doors of houses. But then old Edinburgh was an uncanny place. For a hundred years now some tenements had been left to the rats; everyone knew they were haunted.

The next big robbery was in the August of 1787, when Mr John Carnegie, a grocer in Leith, lost three-and-a-half hundredweights of fine black tea. Again it happened that a part of the stolen goods was recovered: parcels of tea punctuated the length of the western road from Leith to Edinburgh. But the perplexed Procurator-Fiscal put the robbery down to hawkers and vagrants. He could not see the likeness between this and the Royal Exchange banking house job.

On the 29th of October the criminals were again at work in the Royal Exchange in the heart of Edinburgh. This time a fashionable shoe-maker's shop was raided. The following night from the Library in the low-roofed quadrangle of Edinburgh University the College mace went missing. This was three centuries old, of finely wrought silver, and was said to have

B

come from the tomb of the great Bishop Kennedy, the father of the Scottish universities. Now it was the City Chamberlain's turn to offer a reward for information; for the Town Council maintained the University, and the loss of the mace was an affront to its own dignity as well.

If all this opening of locks had something of the supernatural about it, it was clearly no ghostly being who struck at Messrs Inglis and Horner's silk shop in the High Street in the first days of 1788. Five hundred pounds' worth of cambrics, satins and silks vanished. The Procurator-Fiscal's first response was to offer £100 reward for information, a big inducement to an Edinburgh informer. But stronger action was imminent. Now there intervened Ilay Campbell of Succoth, the dour Argyllshire laird who was Lord Advocate and the Government's chief law officer in Scotland. After hurried communication with London (a four-day journey there, a four-day journey back), from Whitehall Lord Sydney, Secretary of State for the Home Department, offered a free pardon for taking part in the crime to any accomplice of the gang who would turn King's evidence.

Whereas, upon the night of the 8th or morning of the 9th of January instant [the proclamation ran], the shop of Messrs Inglis Horner & Co, Silk Mercers in Edinburgh, was broke into, and articles taken therefrom amounting to upwards of £300 value; and as the persons guilty of this robbery have not as yet been discovered, notwithstanding every exertion that has been made, and the offer of £100 of reward for that purpose, his Majesty's most gracious pardon is hereby offered to an accomplice, if there was more than one concerned, who shall, within six months from this date, give such information to William Scott, Procurator-Fiscal for the shire of Edinburgh, as shall be the means of apprehending and securing all or any of the persons guilty of or accessory to the said crime.

For good measure, Mr Scott raised his reward for information to £150, and there was to be a separate reward of twenty guineas for information, even if it did not lead to a conviction. What had not been prevented by the Highlanders of the Town Guard, what the cadies' intelligence network had not unmasked, might be brought to book by dissension among the thieves, could they be persuaded to peach on each other.

But the winter days passed and there was no response. The

THE PRIME OF WILLIAM BRODIE

well of uncertainty in the old town was full to overflowing. No man's property, it seemed, was safe. In the lodgings he had taken high up in the new tenements of St James's Square which looked back across the North Bridge to the Old Town, Robert Burns would hear of the general consternation. Mr Creech had brought out an edition of his poems the previous April. Edinburgh society had taken him up. Trying hard to please, he had written an 'Address to Edinburgh' in his very best English. As 'Caledonia's bard' he had had a northern tour, ducal seats as well as Highland inns for his staging, but he had not obtained the post in government service he so badly needed. Now back in Edinburgh, in his blue coat and buckskin breeches he had become a familiar sight in the town, on his way to convivial suppers, or standing at the nightly book auction at the shop next the Tron, as if hungry for knowledge but with no time to learn.

That January found him a temporary prisoner in his lodgings with a damaged knee, a coach having overturned on the sharp little brae that led up to the Square, so the gossip of the town would be the more likely to reach his ears. However, the poet's ardent thoughts would be elsewhere, directed to the other side of the town and the lady he called Clarinda. She was separated from her unpleasant husband, and in that respectable society the passion that flared up in these winter months between her and the poet was hopeless, soon to subside. Clarinda, incidentally, had sparkle as well as beauty. The praise heaped on the ladies of Edinburgh by young Topham was not all moonshine.

There is little doubt what Mr William Creech thought of it all as he looked down the length of the High Street from the Luckenbooths. Here we must take a closer look at Edinburgh's chief bookseller; for if this is a tale of the two Edinburghs that once lived cheek by jowl, it is also, in a way, the story of two men, Deacon Brodie and William Creech, their lives and actions interwoven in the drama that was to follow. As a shopkeeper and a magistrate of the town Mr Creech would be as anxious as any about the threat to law and order. As arbiter of morals he was sure it was the degeneracy of the times making itself seen.

Emerged from a line of small farmers in Fife, a son of the manse, College educated at Edinburgh, his strict view of things had not even been mellowed by his glimpse of continental ways as tutor to a nobleman on the Grand Tour. From his youth he had been a well-meaning prig. Now an elder of the High Kirk within the old walls of St Giles he had recently written in the *Courant* that twenty years past 'Sunday was strictly observed by all ranks as a day of devotion; and it was disgraceful to be seen in the streets during the time of public worship'. By contrast in the dissolute eighties, he continued, many made Sunday into a day of relaxation, and young people were allowed to stroll about at all hours. The fruits of that evil were all around. 'Religion', he wrote, 'is the only tie that can restrain in any degree the licentiousness either of the rich, or of the lower ranks – when that is lost every breach of morality may be expected.'

As to the general increase in crime it was, thought Mr Creech, the twentyfold increase in the number of brothels over the past score of years which was to blame. Wretched females infested the streets; criminals used the brothels as their rat-holes. There was, too, he wrote, a general decline in standards. Gentlemen were no longer mindful of their position. 'A regular cockpit for the accommodation of this school of gambling and cruelty, where every distinction of rank and character is levelled', now disgraced Edinburgh. In the Assembly rooms minuets were replaced by romps and country-dancing. Too often gentlemen 'reeled from the tavern, flustered with wine, to an assembly of as elegant and beautiful women as any in Europe'. It was all of a piece. Edinburgh was going to the dogs.

There were at least three other men in William Creech, and with the part he – or rather they – play in this story, a word has to be said about them. There was the arbiter of literary taste. The bookshop in the Luckenbooths was the hub of refined thought in Edinburgh, crowded each morning by the *literati*, in the pronunciation of genteel Edinburgh the *leeterati*, attending a sort of literary breakfast which had come to be known as Creech's levee. Professors from the University were there, especially if they were of a philosophical cast of mind. So were lawyers with a taste for letters. Chief of the critics was Henry Mackenzie who had once written a successful novel, but the standard-bearer of correct English was Mr Creech.

He had himself over the years regaled the readers of the *Courant* with a series of essays reflecting his delicate sensibilities.

Then there was Creech the man of business, the moving spirit in the Chamber of Commerce and the town's foremost publisher. Robert Burns had found him not the easiest of men to deal with. Creech's procrastination to publish and slowness to pay had sorely tried him. (But Willie Creech's difficulty was perhaps his inability to see enough merit in the 'heaven-taught', ploughman's pieces. He had been generous enough in paying his friend the Minister of the High Church for his collected sermons.) Lastly, there was convivial Creech. He loved a practical joke. He said he lived only for 'retirement and literary leisure', but he had a passion for company.

In the verses Burns wrote to mark his publisher's visit to London in 1787 there was something of the uncertainty he felt about 'Scotia's darling seat', the would-be speakers of polite English, and Mr Creech.

	O Willie was a witty wight;
uncommon	And had o' things an unco slight;
	Auld Reekie aye he keepit tight,
trim	And trig and Braw;
dress	But now they'll busk her like a fright,
	Willie's awa.

	The stiffest o' them a' he bow'd,
boldest	The bauldest o' them a' he cow'd,
	They durst nae mair than he allow'd,
fellow: gold	We've lost a birkie weel worth good,
	Willie's awa.

	The brethern o' the commerce chaumer,
chamber	May mourn their loss wi' doolfu' clamour,
woeful	He was a dictionar and grammer,
	Amang them a';
	I fear they'll now mak money a stammer,
	Willie's awa.

	Nae mair we see his levee door,
	Philosophers and poets pour,
	And toothy critics by the score,
row	In bloody raw;
Company (Corps)	The adjutant of a' the core,
	Willie's awa.

And so on for several verses more in mock solemnity.

One last word by way of introduction to Bailie Creech. Determined though he was in his stiff-necked way to clear the whores off the streets and pen them in a bridewell under the North Bridge, his bachelor's heart had a genuine concern for the unfortunate girls and their degradation. His effusion in the *Courant* entitled 'Verses for my Tombstone if ever I shall have one by a Prostitute and a Penitent' had a degree of social awareness unusual for his times.

Meanwhile, his adversary the Deacon of the Wrights prospered from the general alarm. The word in the town was that, called in to repair the Inglis and Horner locks, he had been as loud as anyone in denouncing the criminals.

In these opening months of 1788 Mistress Jean Brodie would know, and there would be ladies enough at Mistress Jamie's tea-parties to spread the news, that the Deacon was in hot water at last. For some time now they would have heard that night after night their brother was deep in play with a band of Jemmy Twitchers and Crook-fingered Jacks known as 'The Club' at a certain evil little tavern off the Fleshmarket Close. They could not fail to see that an ugly scar disfigured one of his eyes, and perhaps they had heard that this had been earned in a gaming-table brawl. Now the Deacon had gone too far. He had been caught cheating, and Mr James Hamilton, master of the town's chimney sweeps and climbing boys, had petitioned the Town Council against him.

Hamilton's petition, drawn up in a decorous English which was certainly not his native tongue, said that on a January night he had 'accidentally' met Brodie and his cronies in the tavern at the head of the Fleshmarket Close. They were playing at dice and 'suspecting no fraud or deceit' (as he put it) 'he joined in the amusement and in a short space lost six guineas and some odd shillings'. Baffled by this, he seized the dice and discovered that they were each filled at one corner with lead. So the master sweep's petition to the Town Council was that the Deacon of the Wrights and his gang should be arrested and made to pay damages.

The Deacon's reply, also in genteel English, said that he and his friends 'were innocently amusing themselves with a game at dice over a glass of punch', when Hamilton had intruded himself on their company. 'If false dice were used on that occasion', the reply went on, 'it was unknown to the defenders, as the dice they played with belonged to the house.' Anyhow, it concluded, 'the petitioner is a noted adept in the science of gambling; and it was not very credible that he would have allowed himself to be imposed upon in the manner he had alleged'.

Hamilton's reply, or rather the sarcastic riposte drafted by whatever young advocate he engaged, illuminates the sinister side of the Deacon's nature as it had now become known to his contemporaries.

Mr Brodie knows nothing of such vile tricks! [it jeered]. He never made them his study! Mr Brodie never haunted night-houses, where nothing but the blackest and vilest arts are practised to catch a pigeon! He never was accessory to see or be concerned in fleecing the ignorant, the thoughtless, the young and the unwary, not even made it his study, his anxious study with unwearied concern at midnight hours to haunt the rooms where he thought of meeting with the company from which there was the possibility of fetching from a scurvy sixpence to a hundred guineas! He is unacquainted altogether either with packing or shuffling a set of cards!

And so on to a loaded reference to the cut under the Deacon's eye and how he had come by it, and a final assault on his character and his gang.

There are living instances of men who though born to independence, and enjoying most ample fortune, can intermix with the very lowest class of the multitude, and even court their company, from motives prompted surely by the principles only of rapacity and avarice. . . . What must these men appear to be in the mind of every good person; yet still there are such who demean themselves to these practices, and rather than associate with their equals, will descend to keep company with ostlers, pedlars and stable-boys.

There was, then, a good deal of unease in Edinburgh about the Deacon. The Sheriff's men must have heard of his peculiar ways and of his fellow card-sharpers. So would the other members of the Town Council; but they chose to take no action on the master-sweep's petition. In cosy Edinburgh the scarlet-robed judges of the High Court of Justiciary would likewise know the Deacon's reputation. Yet the following month he was selected by the trial judge to serve as juror in a

murder trial, sitting through a February day in the High Court
of Justiciary within Parliament House to reach a verdict on a
soldier who had discharged his musket at an angry crowd in
the Argyllshire village of Dunoon. In the Scots phrase, the
Deacon was a 'substantial man'. It would take more than a
tavern fracas to shake Sir Lewd.

So to the evening of Wednesday the 8th of March in Chessel's
Court off the Canongate; the bungled break-in at the General
Excise Office, and Mr Bonar's narrow squeak.

Next day, as the news of the attempt on the revenues of
Scotland spread among the shopkeepers, legal gentry, bankers,
and householders with silver to lose, there was alarm and fear.
The mischief-maker who had returned to the door of the Town
Council Chambers the money he had stolen from the bankers
in the Royal Exchange, who had flitted in and out of private
houses and had made off with the University's silver mace, the
mystery man who had become the terror of the half-hundred
shopkeepers on the Bridges, was now tilting at the established
order of things in raiding the revenues of Scotland. The
danger was mortal; and there seemed to be no way of catching
the criminals.

The Thursday and Friday passed with much coming and
going at the Sheriff-Clerk's Office to no good purpose. Then,
late on the Friday evening, an Irishman who sometimes went
by the name of John Brown, sometimes Humphrey Moore,
called there, asking to see Mr William Middleton. Mr Middleton's duties embraced Edinburgh's underworld, and he already
knew Brown. It is more than likely that ever since the advertisement of a free pardon for information about the robberies
he had been waiting for Brown to come forward with an offer
to inform about the whole chain of crime of the past two years.
Now the bubble was about to burst. Just after midnight,
Middleton, Brown in tow, went through the dark streets to the
Procurator-Fiscal's house that Mr Scott might take a statement
from him.

So the offer of a pardon in exchange for evidence had worked
at last. In his years in the criminal underworld of London
Brown *alias* Moore had learned that by English law a King's
Pardon could wipe out all past offence; and he stood much in

need of pardon. For years he had been a wanted man and was still on the run from English justice. Even though the Brodie gang had got clean away from the break-in at Chessel's Court he had now the strongest incentive to come into the haven of the Royal Prerogative: in the cold world outside his own neck was at risk.

At first light of that March morning, Brown led the Sheriff-Clerk's man down the Canongate, through the tumbledown houses of the debtors' sanctuary, past the silent Palace of Holyroodhouse, into the King's Park. There, under the prow of the Salisbury Craigs, he unearthed from under a stone a collection of false keys which in their time had doubtless opened the doors of Inglis and Horner, Bruce the jeweller's, Tapp the goldsmith's, the College Library, the Bank in the Royal Exchange and much else besides.

Brown also named names. His accomplices, Mr Middleton would not be surprised to hear, were one Andrew Ainslie, a shoemaker to trade, who lodged in Burnet's Close off the foot of the High Street; and an Englishman, George Smith, a big gangling fellow with a bulging forehead who kept a grocer's shop in the Cowgate. But Brown did not as yet let slip the name of Deacon Brodie. An important and as yet unsuspected gentleman of the town was involved, he said. This too was perhaps no surprise to Messrs Scott and Middleton. But who could he be? In old Edinburgh of the flickering street lanterns, from which the quality were fast disappearing, there were any number of sharply accentuated individuals of double standards and clandestine ways. Perhaps it was at this stage that the unthinkable possibility of the Deacon's complicity first occurred to them. Brown, Smith and Ainslie frequented Clark's tavern where the master chimney sweep had been fleeced: so did William Brodie.

When it was morning, Smith and his wife were apprehended as they were about to board the Berwick coach. Ainslie too was arrested by the City Guard and committed to the Tolbooth. Under escort Brown was despatched by coach along the high road to England to recover from the fence he had named, a Scotchman called Murray living under the name of Tasker at the Bird in Hand of Chesterfield, the bales of expensive black silk which had been stolen two months past from Messrs Inglis and Horner.

About midday, as gentlemen took their refreshment and the
arrests were being eagerly discussed in every tavern, the
Deacon sallied out of Brodie's Close, striding down the plainstanes of the High Street to the big wooden door of the Tolbooth. To the Keeper he announced that he only wanted to
express his pleasure that the criminals who for so long had
terrorized the town had been taken. And could he, just out of
curiosity, be permitted to see them, perhaps have a word
with them? But the Keeper had been forewarned. No one, not
even a town councillor (especially not a town councillor?)
was to see the prisoners.

Perhaps the Deacon had hoped to induce the Cowgate
grocer and the Burnet's Close shoemaker to hold their tongues.
They would probably have heard him boasting of his part in
springing young Hay from the Tolbooth five years past;
perhaps he thought he could put it into their heads that he
would do the same for them if they would only keep quiet
about his complicity in this latest crime. And the Tolbooth
had quite a name for letting slip its inmates. When he was an
advocate Lord Dunsinnan of Parliament House had procured
the escape of his pretty and adulterous niece to save her neck
and the family's good name. More probably the Deacon's
mind was racing with the excitement of the moment. That
noontide it would be more than he could do to keep to his
workshop and his ledgers. Risk must be piled on risk. He must
steer still closer to the sands to please his wit. Whatever he may
have hoped, whatever the blend of bravado and cunning that
had drawn him to the Tolbooth door, his rebuff there made
up his mind for him.

Next morning, in the early quiet of the Edinburgh Sunday
when nothing moved and not even the slops were collected,
he sent for his foreman as if to give him orders for the coming
week. The Deacon said he would be going out of town for a
few days – and was there, by any chance, word in the town
about what Smith and Ainslie were saying to the Sheriff of
Edinburgh? Straight to the point, as a good Scots foreman
should be, Smith looked his master in the face and said that he
hoped his cocking friends had not involved him in the affairs
at Chessel's Court. Brodie did not answer, but suddenly
invented an errand for his foreman; and when the latter
returned with the new waistcoat and breeches Brodie had said

he needed, their prospective wearer had gone. While Edinburgh was at its stint of Sunday morning devotion within the walls of St Giles, under the Dutch steeple of the Tron Kirk, in the Kirk of the Greyfriars, the Deacon was off down the Canongate, past the pleasure garden of Comely Green, away by the London road, and whirling through East Lothian in a post-chaise.

When Monday came, Brodie's absence from the Edinburgh scene was brushwood to the blaze of rumour. Who else could have fashioned the hoard of false keys the Sheriff's man had unearthed in the King's Park? Who but Brodie had fitted new locks to the High Street shops when the causeway was relaid? The speculation was not long in reaching the newly committed prisoners of the Tolbooth, for all that they were held *incommunicado*. After an agony of indecision George Smith made up his mind; and he told the Keeper that he was ready to make a clean breast of things to the Sheriff. At last Brodie's complicity was to come into the open. But it still was a thunderclap over the town when that week's *Courant* was read in the high lands and douce dwellings.

The depredations that have been committed by housebreakers in and about this city for this some time past [it said], have been no less alarming than the art with which they have been executed, and the concealment that has attended them has been surprising. From a discovery, however, just made, there is reason to hope that a stop will soon be put to such acts of atrocious villainy.

Then came the organ-blast. It sounds like Mr Creech at his best. It probably was.

With what amazement must it strike every friend to virtue and honesty to find that a person is charged with a crime of the above nature who very lately held a distinguished rank among his fellow-citizens? With what pity and compunction must we view the unfortunate victim who falls a sacrifice to justice for having violated the laws of his country, to which violation he was perhaps impelled by necessity, when rank, ease, and opulence are forfeited in endeavouring to gratify the most sordid avarice? For to what other cause than avarice can be imputed the late robbery committed upon the Excise Office, what excuse from necessity can be pled for a man in the enjoyment of thousands, who will run the risk of life, honour and reputation in order to attain the unlawful possession of what could in a very trifling degree add to his supposed happiness.

With it was an advertisement from the Sheriff-Clerk's Office.

TWO HUNDRED POUNDS OF REWARD

Whereas William Brodie, a considerable House-Carpenter and Burgess of the City of Edinburgh, has been charged with being concerned in breaking into the General Excise Office for Scotland, and stealing from the Cashier's Office there a sum of money – and as the said William Brodie has either made his escape from Edinburgh, or is still concealed about that place – a REWARD OF ONE HUNDRED AND FIFTY POUNDS STERLING is hereby offered to any person who will produce him alive at the Sheriff Clerk's Office, Edinburgh, or will secure him, so as he may be brought there within a month from this date; and FIFTY POUNDS STERLING MORE, payable upon his conviction, by William Scott, procurator-fiscal for the shire of Edinburgh.

Smith told Mr Archibald Cockburn, Laird of Cockpen and Sheriff-Depute for the shire of Edinburgh, that he had been a hawker in the south of England, travelling around the southern counties with a horse, a cart and his wife. Two years past he had come to Edinburgh. Why he did not say; but a dealer in shady business would have to keep on the move. Arrived in Edinburgh in that year when Mr Burns was the talk of the town, he quickly made his presence felt at Henderson's cockpit in the Grassmarket, the broad *place* below the Castle Rock. There, like being drawn to like, he met Brown the Irishman on the run, and Ainslie the cobbler. Here too, down on his luck, he met Brodie, who having sized up his man, observed that 'several things could be done in this place, if prudently managed' and that 'they should lay their heads together for that purpose'.

So the Deacon began to use Smith for the selection of targets in the town, and the criminal quartet was formed of Brown the Irish thug, Smith the Englishman, Ainslie the Scotch thief and the Deacon himself. One target had been the Library in the low-roofed quadrangle of the old University. This they visited, town councillors being the dispensers of University patronage, and Brodie pointed out the famous Bishop Kennedy silver mace, saying out the corner of his mouth 'that they must have it'. And so they did; the Deacon provided the key (for he had fitted the lock) and Ainslie made the snatch.

Now continued the series of crimes which had perplexed Mr Cockburn and terrified the shopkeepers. Smith's description of the doing of two shops close by the new North Bridge was a fair sample of the lot. (The voice was Smith's but the hand was the Sheriff-Clerk's. Smith could not write.) Here was the style of the Brodie gang as they flitted from the new shops on Bridge Street to the gambling den a hundred yards away down Fleshmarket Close, to the Deacon's spacious home off the Lawnmarket, to Michael Henderson's stables in the Grassmarket. It was all within the radius of a half mile and under the noses of the Town Guard.

In the month of November 1786 [said Smith], Mr Brodie and I had laid a plan to break into a hardware shop on Bridge Street, belonging to Davidson McKain. So we went there one night with a parcel of false keys and a small crow iron, and opened the door, by unlocking the padlock and lock with the false keys. After this we went and hid the false keys and crow iron, in case any of these articles should be found upon us and then returned to the shop. I was to go into the shop, and Mr Brodie to watch at the outside of the door. I carried with me a dark lanthorn, which I lighted. Our intention was only to look at the goods, but not to carry them off that night.

I remained in the shop for about half an hour; and, after being some time there Brodie called out, 'What makes you stay so long, are you taking an inventory of the shop?'

Smith's matter-of-fact narrative continues, the unemotional report of the professional thief, wanting altogether the romance with which the Deacon clothed his night-life; he saw Brodie only as the gang's hard-fisted boss.

I only brought away with me that night seventeen steel watch chains, and a small red pocket-book. The steel chains I afterwards sold along with some other goods of my own to an auctioneer, and the pocket-book I afterwards made a present of to Michael Henderson, stabler in Grassmarket, his daughter.

Mr Brodie and I afterwards, in about a fortnight, went back to rob McKain's shop completely, and opened the door as formerly, went in, and left Brodie to watch without; but I was not a few minutes in the shop, when I heard a person in the room immediately below rise out of his bed, and come towards the door. At this I pulled up the shop-door, and ran straight into the street, without carrying anything with me. I found Brodie had fled; and on going up to the main street, I found Mr Brodie standing at the head of the entry into the Old Green Market.

A little after this, Mr Brodie and I walked arm in arm down Bridge Street, in order to see what we could observe about the shop; and, in passing down the street, we saw a man looking out at the door immediately under McKain's shop, and a guard soldier standing opposite, at the head of the stair which goes down to the Fleshmarket. So we passed on along the Bridge, and afterwards went to our several homes, as nothing could be done further that night.

Mr Brodie then told me that the shop at the head of Bridge Street, belonging to Messrs Bruce, would be a very proper shop for breaking into, as it contained valuable goods, and he knew the lock would be easily opened, as it was a plain lock, his men having lately altered that shop door, at the lowering of the streets. The plan of breaking into this shop was accordingly concerted between us and we agreed to meet on the evening of the 24th of December 1786, being a Saturday, at the house of James Clark vintner in the head of the Fleshmarket Close, where we generally met with other company to gamble. Having met there, we played at the game of hazard, till I lost all my money; but at this time Brodie was in luck, and gaining money. I often asked Brodie to go with me on our own business; but Brodie, as he was gaining money declined going, and desired me to stay a little, and he would go with me. However I turned impatient, as it was near four in the morning, and the time for doing our business was going, so left the room, and went by myself to Messrs Bruce's shop, when I opened the door with false keys, and, after getting in, lighted a dark lanthorn, and took out of the show-boxes or glasses on the counter, and from the inside of the windows, ten watches, five of them gold, three silver, and two metal, with the whole rings, lockets, and other jewellery and gold trinkets in the show-boxes, all which I put into two old black stockings, and carried them to the stable of Michael Henderson in the Grassmarket, where I hid them under some rubbish below the manger, and afterwards went home to my own room in the Grassmarket.

I stayed there till near eight in the morning, and then went up to Mr Brodie's house. When the maid told me that Mr Brodie was in bed I then left my name, and said I wanted to see him, and thereafter returned home to my own room. After staying there some time, Mr Brodie came and called for me, when I told him what I had done, and desired Mr Brodie to stay there till I would go for the goods. So I went to the stable, and brought the two black stockings, containing the goods, and poured them out upon a bed in a closet off his room, and then said to Mr Brodie, 'You see what luck I have been in; you might have been there; but as you did not go, you cannot expect a full share; but there are the goods, pick out what you choose for yourself.' Upon this Brodie took a gold seal, a gold watch-key set with garnet stones, and two gold rings. Mr Brodie and I went twice over the goods, in order to ascertain their value; and I, who am skilled in articles in that line, was of opinion they would have cost Messrs Bruces about L. 350 Sterling.

After this, the goods were again put into the black stockings, and carried back to Michael Henderson's stable; and, in the course of that day, being Sunday, Mr Brodie and I frequently passed Messrs Bruce's shop-door, to see in what situation the door stood, and to learn if the robbery had been discovered; and nothing appearing, I proposed to Mr Brodie to go back that night in order to sweep the shop clean; but Mr Brodie objected to this, saying, that a discovery might have been made, and a watch set to entrap them; on which account we desisted from the attempt.

After this, Mr Brodie and I had several meetings, consulting about the safest way to dispose of the goods; and, upon the Tuesday evening, it was concerted between us, that I should go off next day for England with the goods; and at that time Mr Brodie gave me five guineas and a half to carry my expenses on the road; and, to evade suspicion, I set out early next morning, and travelled on foot as far as Dunbar, where I took the mail coach, and went to Chesterfield in England, and there sold the whole goods taken out of Messrs Bruce's shop, except what Mr Brodie got, for L. 105 Sterling, to John Tasker, alias Murray, who I knew, had been banished from Scotland. I sent a twenty-pound note of this money in a letter to Mr Brodie, informing him of the sale, and desiring him to pay himself what I had borrowed, and supply my wife with money till my return. I stayed for some weeks in England, during which time I had several letters from Mr Brodie; and, on my return, gave to Mr Brodie three ten-pound notes more of the money to keep for me and to prevent suspicion by my having so much money about me, which money Brodie gave me as I wanted it, but gained a great part of it at play.

It was Brodie who suggested 'the doing of Inglis and Horner's shop, as the goods there were very rich and valuable and a small bulk of them carried off would amount to a large sum'. And as with the doing of Bruce's shop, it was on Sunday mornings when the streets were deserted that the two studied the pad and stock lock of the shop near the Cross. These were complicated locks; with a touch of naïve pride, Smith told Mr Cockburn that he had succeeded in making a key to open them after the Deacon had made a botch of it.

Also bearing the stamp of Brodie planning had been the concealment of the loot from Messrs Inglis and Horner until it could be got away by the Berwick carrier to their English fence. For this they had rented a stable at one of the fashionable houses in George's Square, next door to the Lord Justice Clerk.

It was Brodie too who had planned the big job, the break-in, at the General Excise Office of Scotland. He had a relative who often had to go there, a Mr Corbett from Stirling whose business was probably the payment of the new excise duty afflicting the whisky distilleries in the Carse of Stirling. Brodie, said Smith, got into the way of accompanying Mr Corbett to the big building in Chessel's Court, there to watch how the cashier put the money away in his desk. Sometimes Smith would also accompany them. One day his sharp eyes noted that the key to the building's big outside door hung from a nail in the passageway within. In a flash, he had some putty out of a box (which he just happened to have in his pocket) and clapped it round the key. Back at the workshop down Brodie's Close, the Deacon then made a drawing from the putty impression and cut a duplicate.

But the Excise Office cashier must have been more careful than the Deacon had reckoned. Smith described the frenzy of their search of his desk on the night of the break-in; it missed the hidden drawer where £600 of revenue money lay, and yielded up only the petty cash. He also told how that night Brodie had carried in his greatcoat pocket a wig of his worthy father for use as a disguise should need arise; how the ways of the office night watchman had been observed for days beforehand; and how a spur, as if torn from a boot, had been left on the floor, this to suggest that the robbers had come from a distance. And he said that the gang had gone armed with Brodie's pistols. Little Mr Bonar disturbing them at their work had been lucky not to be pistolled down.

George Smith began to 'sing' to the Sheriff-Depute on the Monday morning; that afternoon he accompanied a posse of Sheriff's officers which, no doubt, greatly adding to Miss Jean's consternation, searched the big house off Brodie's Close. In the bottom of a vent used as a fireplace for melting glue they unearthed a pair of pistols wrapped in a green cloth. In the necessary house (the Brodie house had modern sanitation) they found part of a night lantern such as housebreakers would use; the rest was concealed with the gamecocks in the pen. Then Smith took the Sheriff's men to an old wall above the stinking swamp of the Nor' Loch and showed them the hole where the gang had hidden the false keys, irons and crows used in the break-in at Chessel's Court. The same afternoon the town was combed for Brodie. Remembering the Deacon's supposed part in young Hay's escape of five years past they searched the kirkyard of the Greyfriars; and that night Mr George Williamson, the King's Messenger for Scotland, was deputed by the Sheriff to take up his trail along the London road.

At Dunbar they remembered the gentleman who had arrived from Edinburgh on the Sunday afternoon. At Newcastle, Williamson was told his quarry had taken the 'Flying Mercury' post-coach to York and then to London. So to London he went to seek out its coachman. His passenger from Newcastle, said the coachman of the 'Flying Mercury', had got off at Moorfields, had not gone on to the terminus at the Bull and Mouth. Williamson presented himself to Sir Sampson Wright, chief magistrate at Bow Street, and explained his business. But Sir Sampson could not help. A lone Scotsman in the wickedness of London, Williamson searched the billiard rooms and cockpits for sight of a sallow-faced man with a queer way of walking and a scar under one eye. Then he went on to the Channel ports. It was all to no avail. By the end of March the King's Messenger was back in Edinburgh. The Deacon had got clean away and there was little chance of his ever being brought to justice. But to be on the safe side, his Edinburgh friends retained the services of Henry Erskine, Dean of the Faculty of Advocates and the best pleader at the Scots Bar.

Glacial Edinburgh winter became chilly Edinburgh spring, and the city turned to other things. There was much to talk about. The whisky distillers continued to be in deep difficulties. They had distilled more of John Barleycorn than even Scotland could drink and had failed to find a market for the spirit in London, the English gin distillers undercutting them; so that April was marked by bankruptcies in the Lothians and a shaking of heads at the noontime gathering round the Cross.

The city fathers would also be concerned at the unquiet that was abroad. To their minds there was far too much questioning of the traditional right of town councils to run the royal

burghs of Scotland as they pleased; too much criticism of the
Dundas grip on the Scottish members of Parliament and on all
Scottish patronage. It was true that under the time-honoured
system whereby each town council perpetuated its own exist-
ence some regrettable practices had crept in. Some provosts
and magistrates had disposed of the handsome patrimonies of
burgh lands to line their own pockets. But the system had kept
Scotland steady. As to the conduct of the Scotch members of
Parliament at Westminster, it was a fact that they existed only
to do the bidding of Henry Dundas and Ilay Campbell ('The
Lord Advocate should always be a tall man,' said one. 'We
Scotch members always vote with him and we need therefore
to be able to see him in a Division.') But why not? Sensible
men would be content that Henry Dundas was Mr Pitt's
Treasurer of the Navy as well as Keeper of the Scottish Signet
and good at finding posts in India, commissions in the Navy,
for young Scots of family.

The legal round went on as ever. The coaches of Lords
Braxfield and Swinton lumbered along the Linlithgow road;
their Lordships were off on the spring circuit which would
take them to Stirling, there to hang a Falkirk forger, through
the hills to Inverary, and then to Glasgow. Lords Eskgrove
and Hailes departed for the rigours of the northern circuit,
half-made roads and rivers to cross; Lords Stonefield and
Henderland to dispense justice and hospitality in the Borders.

Looking around them in the lengthening days of April, the
people of Edinburgh could take a proper pride in what was
being achieved. There was, that year, a new piped water
supply from the springs of Comiston. Now more than ever the
city could rebut its ill-name for uncleanliness. There was still
only one way for disposal from the high lands. The time-
honoured customs still held good.

After ten o'clock in the evening, it is Fortune favours you if a
Chamber-pot with excrements etc. is not thrown on your head,
if you are walking the streets; it is then not a little diversion to a
stranger, to hear all Passers-by cry out, with a loud voice, sufficient
to reach the tops of the houses (which are generally six or seven
stories high in the front of the High Street) *Hoad yare Hoand*, and
means do not throw till I am past . . . as for example Hold your
Hand in Blackfryar's Land; this, with variation is the common
cry all over the streets at ten o'clock at night and after.

But this was only the first precipitate stage in the profitable matter of refuse disposal. The Town Council now leased the cleansing of the streets to a private contractor for £500 a year, Sundays excepted the causeway was thoroughly washed early each morning before people were abroad.

There were other improvements. A new green market had been opened at the foot of Halkerston's Wynd, and there was an end to the clutter of stalls and the stink of decaying cabbage in the High Street below the Tron. New shops were opening daily on the bridge over the Cowgate now completed. It was a city of handsome buildings, Adam's honey coloured Register House across the North Bridge complementing Heriot's Hospital which, then as now, schooled the Edinburgh young 'till they are fit for apprenticeships or to go to University'.

In the first days of May, Smith and Ainslie nearly got clean away from the Tolbooth prison. It was a bold attempt. In the warren of the Tolbooth the two were kept well apart, Ainslie's cell being on the top floor under the building's ancient roof. Experienced housebreaker that he was, Smith saw that something could be done with his slop-bucket. Its iron handle he fashioned into a picklock, the hoops round the bucket into a rudimentary saw. With these one night he took his cell door off its hinges; he climbed the turnpike stairs and opened the door of Ainslie's cell. Then, a hundred feet of bedsheet rope in readiness, the two cut their way through the roof. But the nights of May are short in Edinburgh. At first light they were still at work, some of the roofing slates clattered on the plainstanes far below, and the alarm was raised. Their bid for freedom had narrowly failed, though Sheriff Cockburn must have felt that his own reputation for maintaining law and order had had another narrow squeak.

The stir this caused died down. Speculation about the vanished Deacon was laid aside as the capital turned to the yearly splash that went with the General Assembly of the Church of Scotland. Edinburgh filled up with clergymen from all the airts; and in the afternoon they filled the Theatre Royal where a new play, *The Follies of Fashion*, was badly received.

The city guard lining the street, the Earl of Leven, Lord High Commissioner, with his suite walked from his lodgings

in a High Street tavern across the causeway to St Giles. There
he was received by the magistrates in their robes. Then they
entered one of the three kirks into which St Giles was parti-
tioned; and there, as the *Edinburgh Magazine* put it, 'an excellent sermon' was preached by the retiring Moderator.

There followed in the presence of the Lord High Commissioner a week of Church business and debate under the roof
of St Giles. Though the ministers had to be dined, a bottle of
port to each two reverend throats, at its salary of £2000 a
year the job was a handsome piece of government patronage.
A sound Dundas man, Leven had been reappointed Commissioner year after year for so long that he had enquired if
he could not simply have the post for life.

And it was in Assembly week that word came to Edinburgh
of Deacon Brodie's whereabouts.

That the Deacon's friends should have engaged as counsel the
Honourable Henry Erskine, brother to the Earl of Buchan,
was a measure of his eminence at the Scottish bar and of his
client's desperate plight. As befitted an Edinburgh town
councillor the Deacon was a Dundas man, committed to the
predominant Tory interest for which Henry Dundas was
Scottish viceroy. Erskine by contrast was the acknowledged
leader of the Scottish Whigs, presided over the Prince of
Wales's (opposition) household in Scotland, and as champion
of the cause of burgh reform sought to break the Dundas grip
on parliament and patronage, the 'outs' wishing to become the
'ins', as always. But Harry Erskine had no equal as a pleader.
His distinctive delivery had driven out of fashion the traditional, whining style of speaking. He reasoned in wit, and that
was something new in Parliament House. If anyone could
persuade a jury to acquit the Deacon it was he.

Politics apart, and politics had not yet wrecked the social
life of old Edinburgh, everyone from the Duchess of Gordon
to the doorkeeper at Parliament House thought the world of
Harry Erskine. The third Lord Erskine had fallen at Flodden;
his grandson had died in the slaughter at Pinkie; so he had the
patrician's self-assurance to stand up to the illiberal ways of
lesser men. Tall and fair-haired, with big eyes and strong
features, at the concerts in St Cecilia's Hall off the Cowgate,

he played the violin to an admiring audience. He was an excellent dancer. His habit of playing with words conveyed clearly his humorous, quizzical view of life. He was something of a poet too; a piece he had written deploring the emigration of the Highlanders from their native glens and islands had been much admired by the *literati* at Creech's shop:

Fast by the margin of a mossy rill,
That wandered gurgling down a heath-clad hill,
An ancient shepherd stood, opprest with woe,
And eye'd the ocean flood that foamed below,
Where gently rocking on the rising tide,
A ship's unwonted form was seen to ride . . .

And so on, to a swipe at all evicting landlords:

Another lord now rules these wide domains,
The avaricious tyrant of the plains,
Far, far from hence he revels life away,
In guilty pleasures our poor means must pay.

But he was genuinely warm-hearted and generous; had helped the visiting balloonist Lunardi get off the ground; and on his visit to Edinburgh had been kindly attentive to the poet Burns who wrote such interesting verse in the Scotch vernacular. He kept a smart yellow coach and black horses for travel from his Edinburgh home to the handsome low house he had built in the Italian style down by the rocky gorge of the River Almond ('But you have no prospect,' complained his brother at its lack of a view. 'You forget, my dear David, I have always the prospect of your estate.')

One day during Assembly week, to Harry Erskine's new house in Princes Street there came one John Geddes, a tobacconist in the Lothian village of Mid Calder. The tale Geddes had to tell was that he had seen Brodie take a ship to the Continent.

Returning to Scotland from a visit to London in March, said Geddes, he and his wife had gone abroad the *Endeavour* sloop of the Carron Iron Company. Off Gravesend she had cast anchor while the captain went on shore to muster a crew; and late that night he had returned with two gentlemen of the Carron Company escorting an additional passenger. This newcomer was unwell, and dressed in a shabby old blue greatcoat, but Captain Dent had given him a bed by the fire in the state-room, and straightway the *Endeavour* had set sail. The sloop had then run aground on the mudbanks of Tilbury Point and stuck fast there for ten days. All ˎthis while the stranger kept himself to himself, going ashore only once to buy some milk for his sore throat. The Geddeses could get out of him no more than that his name was 'Dixon'.

Free at last from the mud, the *Endeavour* had made for the open sea, but at this point 'Dixon' had handed the Captain sealed orders from the gentlemen of the Carron Company. An inquisitive fellow, Geddes had tried without success to have a sight of them. Captain Dent had then changed course, steering not for Leith but for the Low Countries. Here 'Dixon' had set off for Ostend in a skiff, but not before he had handed the Mid Calder tobacconist a parcel of letters which he asked him to deliver for him when he reached Scotland. It was these letters which Geddes now wished Erskine to see, for he had already opened the package, read them, and had spent the past three weeks in an ecstasy of indecision while he tried to make up his mind what to do. At last and belatedly he called at No. 53 Princes Street. Perhaps he thought that there might be something in it for him if he now gave them to Brodie's counsel.

Unfortunately for Geddes, if indeed he thought to profit from the letters, Harry Erskine was also Dean of the Faculty of Advocates. When he read the letters he saw at once that he must have nothing to do with them. They were for the Sheriff's eyes only and so he sent Mr Geddes packing.

There were three letters from Brodie, each different masks of the man. The first, dated 'Flushing Tuesday 8th April 1788, 12 o'clock forenoon,' was to Matthew Sheriff, his brother-in-law, the St James's Square upholsterer. It admitted nothing, was a little droll in tone – 'this afternoon I will set off by water for Bruges and then for Ostend. So I begin my travels where most gentlemen leave off' – and complained ruefully of the old clothes he had had to wear to make good his escape, 'my wardrobe is all on my back'.

A businesslike, brother-in-law-like letter, it asked that the tools of his trade, 'my quadrant and spirit level – they lie in a triangular box in my old bedroom – my brass-cased measuring line and three foot rule' be sent on 'to the care of the Rev. Mr Mason at New York'. An American clergyman was to set him up in the New World; a Scotch one, the Revd Mr Nairn, had made possible his sudden getaway from Edinburgh, so the letter implied. This clergyman and the brother-in-law had been left in charge of the Brodie finances. 'And I hope to have a long letter from each of you', the Deacon concluded, as if his intended voyage across the Atlantic were the most natural thing in the world, 'and one from my sister, Jeany, and your's will include your wife's'. But there was a postscript. 'Let my name and destination be a profound secret, for fear of bad consequences.'

The second letter was to his crony, Michael Henderson the Grassmarket stabler and owner of the cockpit which had been the haunt of the Brodie gang.

Were I to write to you all that has happened to me [he wrote cheerfully] and the hairbreadth escapes I made from a well-scented pack of bloodhounds, it would make a small volume.

I left Edinburgh Sunday the 9th and arrived in London Wednesday the 12th where I remained snug and safe in the house of an old female friend, (whose care for me I shall never forget and only wish I may ever have it in my power to reward her sufficiently,) within five hundred yards of Bow Street.

From this hideout with his London doxy, the Deacon had gone out on the town, while Williamson the Sheriff's Officer from Edinburgh was searching the gambling dens and cockpits of London: 'I saw Mr Williamson twice, but although countrymen commonly shake hands when they meet from home, yet I did not choose to make so free with him.'

In the slang of the times, a 'flash man' was a crook. In a passage which hints at friends in the Sheriff-Clerk's Office and goes some way towards explaining Brodie's long undetected criminal run in Edinburgh, he went on to say:

My female gave me great uneasiness by introducing a flash man to me, but she assured me he was a true man, and he proved himself so, not withstanding the great reward, and was useful to me. I saw my picture six hours before exhibited to public view, and my intelligence of what was doing at Bow Street was as good as ever I had in Edinburgh.

The shipboard life in the *Endeavour*, he said, 'agrees vastly well with me'. (In fact he had had a sore throat.) As to what was going on in Edinburgh: 'I beg you will write me, or dictate a letter, and let it be a very long one, giving me an account of

what is likely to become of poor Ainslie, Smith and his wife.'
As to Brown, he was a 'designing villain', and 'I make no doubt
but he is now in high favour with Mr Cockburn . . . may God
forgive him all his crimes and falsehoods. I hope in a short time
to be in Edinburgh, and confute personally many false asper-
sions made against me by him and others.'

Then on to cockfighting. He must be told how the Brodie
black cock fared at the big match at Henderson's pit on the
7th of April. Finally instructions about the routing of correspondence; his worthy foreman was to carry any letter to Miss
Jeany 'who will take care that it be conveyed safe to me wherever I may happen to be at the time'. And so 'my best compli-
ments to Mrs Henderson', and an assurance that a sum of two
guineas he was owing her would be paid as soon as possible.

The third letter, also to Henderson, was from Brodie, the
family man.

Dear Michael,
   I am very uneasy on account of Mrs Grant and my three children
by her; they will miss me more than any other in Scotland. May
God, in his infinite goodness, stir up some friendly aid for their
support, for it is not in my power at present to give them the smallest
assistance. Yet I think they will not absolutely starve in a Christian
land where their father once had friends, and who was always
liberal to the distressed.

Then he gave his views on what should become of his
daughters. Jean the youngest should be sent to friends at
Aberdeen, 'and I will order a yearly board to be paid for her,
perhaps six pounds per annum'. Cecill, his eldest, should be
apprenticed to a milliner, 'but I wish she could learn a little writing and arithmetic first. I wish to God some of my friends would
take some charge of Cecill: she is a fine, sensible girl, considering
the little opportunity she had for improvement.' He ended with
a postscript: 'Do not show this scroll to any but your wife.'

Harry Erskine would give a sympathetic and quizzical smile
at these letters, as he told Geddes to put them in the Sheriff's
hands. He would know the Deacon well – he would think he
had known the Deacon well – from long past; and he would
have imagination enough to wonder at the man. The Sheriff's
reaction was singleminded. Within an hour he had the Procurator-Fiscal on the road to West Lothian that he might bring

the Mid Calder tobacconist back to Edinburgh for examination. The shipboard letters Geddes had so belatedly brought to notice held no admission of the author's part in the Chessel's Court affair or in the earlier crimes. They did offer the authorities a slender hope of seeking him out. It was much more likely by now that Brodie would be halfway across the Atlantic; and once he had set foot in the newly established United States of America he could cock a snook at Mr Cockburn and the paraphernalia of the law. But the hunt was worth a try; and so the Lord Advocate moved the Secretary of State in London to write to the British Consul at Ostend, who in turn engaged John Daly, an Irishman living there. It may have been Daly's business to scrutinize travellers from England, for he remembered seeing a man who went by the name of Dixon at the house of one John Bacon, a vintner at Ostend.

Mr Bacon had kept the letter of introduction 'Mr Dixon' had brought from the Captain of the *Endeavour*. 'The bearer, John Dixon', wrote Captain Dent, tongue in cheek, 'was going passenger with me to New York, but being taken sick had a desire to be landed at Ostend. . . . I recommend him to your care being a countryman and a stranger. On my account I hope you'll render him every service in your power.' In the event Mr Bacon did his guest the disservice of telling Daly that his guest had gone to Holland. So on to Amsterdam the Irishman went. There two Jews who attended to passengers arriving by *schuit* remembered the shabbily dressed Scot with a black trunk for baggage. For a small sweetener, they pointed out the alehouse where he had taken up his quarters. Brodie was discovered hiding in the cupboard of an upstairs room. Daly made him his prisoner, and pending extradition, he was lodged in the Stadthouse at Amsterdam. Then the Irishman went to London to collect his reward.

Mr Bacon, the Ostend vintner, remembered Brodie the more clearly because the Deacon had been with him on the 4th of June; and the King's Birthday was celebrated wherever Britons gathered together.

In Edinburgh, as in every royal burgh of Scotland, the 4th of June was well marked. From early morning the street wells were clad with greenery, the lamp brackets with broom; and it fell to the boys of Heriot's Hospital to garland with flowers the statue of King Charles in the Parliament Close. Everyone took a holiday; at noon the Union flag was run up above Edinburgh Castle and the guns fired a royal salute, the bangs reverberating from Salisbury Craigs and Calton Hill, the smoke drifting over the roof-tops of the old town. Then the red-nosed Donalds of the City Guard formed up in the Parliament Close and everyone who mattered made his way to the Parliament House for an evening's drinking at the town's expense. As each toast was given within (and there were many, for the health of each of King George's numerous progeny had to be drunk), to the cheers of the mob the Guard let off *feux de joie* (in Inverness, lacking a town guard, the fire engines were employed, celebratory jets of water instead of volleys from muskets). Soon the uneven paving of the great hall was strewn with broken glass. Outside, standards of behaviour also slipped as the Edinburgh apprentices' long day of idleness was followed by an evening of mischief-making. Fireworks flew about. So did dead cats, aimed with precision at the departing guests. A good time was had by all.

On the first day of July Mr Groves, a Public Office Clerk from Bow Street, left London to bring the Deacon back. He kept a journal of the jaunt, on which he was accompanied by a Bow Street officer with the unusual name of Carpmeal.

By the afternoon of the 2nd of July, the Harwich packet was standing out from land; by nine of the summer evening she was halfway across to Holland. Then the wind dropped and by noon the next day she was twelve miles off Helvoetsluys in a dead calm. The ship's long-boat rowed ashore, then dumped Messrs Groves and Carpmeal, their few fellow passengers and the mailbags beside the sand dunes. Helvoetsluys was still several miles off and the party spent an exasperating, thirsty afternoon going from farm to farm in search of transport. 'At three in the morning, in an open post waggon with heavy rain, thunder and lightning', they reached The Hague.

The problem was how to secure Brodie's extradition. Mr Groves would be armed with the Procurator-Fiscal's description of the Deacon, 'about five feet four inches, about forty-eight years of age but looks rather younger than he is, broad at the

shoulders and very small over the loins', and so on. But this
would not be enough if Brodie refused to say who he was. The
Dutch magistrates would be sticklers for the law; they might
require an application to be made to their States-General;
and Britain only a few years past had been at war with Holland.

Mr Rich, the British consul at Amsterdam, thought he had
the answer. A Mr Duncan, a clergyman from Aberdeen, was
on a visit to his son-in-law, the minister at the Scots kirk, and
Mr Rich had met him. Even at this distance from Scotland the
Brodie affair must have been the subject of discussion: in
conversation Mr Duncan had mentioned to the consul that
eight years past he had seen the Deacon in Edinburgh. Straight
away the gentlemen from Bow Street waited on worthy Mr
Duncan and Mr Gerard, his son-in-law.

Mr Duncan [Groves noted in his journal], seemed willing to
identify Brodie, but on being called out into another room by Mr
Gerard and his wife, on his return Mr Duncan said . . . if an oath
was required he would not. Saw then a manifest reluctance in Mr
Duncan and had no doubt his daughter and the parson would
endeavour to persuade him to decline troubling himself in the
matter. No mischief but a woman or a priest in it – here both.

Nothing could be done over the weekend as the magistrates
had gone to their country houses. Mr Groves's unease increased.
'As Mr Duncan lodged in the same tavern with me,' he wrote,
'I had frequent opportunities of conversation with him, and
could plainly see a sorrow for what he had said, and a wish to
retract.' Scots abroad stick together.

At ten o'clock on the Tuesday Mr Groves presented himself
at the Stadthouse. Mr Duncan had also been summoned.
Brodie was brought in for examination.

'What is your name?' asked the Chief Magistrate.

'John Dixon,' said the prisoner.

'That is the name you go by here. But is not your real name
William Brodie?'

'My Lords, I stand here and claim the protection of the laws
of this country which require two witnesses on oath to prove
me William Brodie.'

'You shall have the protection of the laws of this country,
but they do not require two oaths to identify you. It requires
that the Magistrate shall be satisfied you are the same man.'

Here Groves intervened. 'I beg leave he may be asked if he is not a native of Edinburgh,' he said.

'Are you a native of Edinburgh?' said the Chief Magistrate to Brodie.

'I have been at Edinburgh,' he replied.

'Is he a Deacon of Edinburgh,' put in Groves, his anxiety growing.

'I claim the protection of the laws,' said the prisoner.

Then Mr Duncan from Aberdeen was put to the question.

'I'm only a visitor here,' he said, 'I do believe and I have no doubt, that he is the same man. But I won't swear it. I'll take no oath.'

At this, says Groves, the Magistrates 'expostulated' but Mr Duncan would not be budged.

A simple ruse by the Chief Magistrate ended this entr'acte. The prisoner was recalled.

'Have you a father?' asked the Magistrate.

'None.'

'But you had a father?'

'Yes.'

'Was not his name Brodie?'

'There are more Brodies than one.'

'Then by that,' said the Magistrate, 'you confess your name is Brodie?'

The game was nearly up. 'A *lapsus linguae*, my Lord,' smiled William Brodie.

The *Journal* continues:

At four was sent for to the Stadthouse, where there was a prodigious crowd, two carriages and four guides, with four horses in each carriage; and the prisoner being properly secured, we put him into one, and got to Helvoet without much interruption next day at one o'clock. Packet sailed at five.

The Deacon was put under constant watch by the ship's crew; his hands and arms confined. Perhaps they felt some sympathy for him. 'On Thursday night, eleven o'clock, we arrived at Harwich – supped – set off immediately, and arrived next day at noon at Sir Sampson Wright's.'

No doubt Groves was given the praise that was his due: for at last 'Brodie confessed he was the person advertised'.

On the 17th of July, Brodie came back to Edinburgh. In the

post-chaise Mr Groves of Bow Street was with him; so was Williamson, the King's Messenger for Scotland, who had in vain searched the London cockpits and gaming houses three months past. The Deacon was in high spirits and full of his Dutch adventures. He said that at Amsterdam (was it this that delayed his passage to New York?) he had struck up a friendship with another fugitive Scot, a forger whose speciality had been the imitation of Bank of Scotland notes. And before his appearance at Sheriff Cockburn's house at the Meadows, Brodie insisted that the King's Messenger shave him.

There was no regret at the twin lunacies of trusting the Mid Calder tobacconist with the packets of letters which disclosed his whereabouts, and of delaying the passage to America which would have taken him out of range of any Bow Street runner. It was as if he were now coming home in triumph, the skill with which he had managed his double life for so many years now obvious to everyone. Indeed, it was almost as if the passage to America would have been too easy a way out. Now Edinburgh would see how Brodie–Macheath would outface even the most desperate danger.

He was served with a copy of the indictment on which he was to stand trial, but he was put down neither by this, nor by his close confinement in the murky Tolbooth. Day and night he was watched by two soldiers of the City Guard. He was not even allowed a knife and fork to eat his dinner. And there was no means to cut his toenails.

The nails of my toes and fingers are not quite so long as Nebuchadnezzar's are said to have been [he wrote from the Town Council's prison to a fellow councillor], although long enough for a Mandarine, and much longer than I find convenient. I have tried several experiments to remove this evil without effect, which no doubt you'll think says little for your ward's ingenuity: and I have the mortification to perceive the evil daily increasing.

Dear Sir [he continued], as I intend seeing company abroad in a few days, I beg as soon as convenient you'll take this matter under consideration . . . if not disagreeable to you, I'll be happy to see you. You'll be sure to find me at home, and all hours are equally convenient.

About the middle of July 'the public of Edinburgh', as the *Edinburgh Magazine* put it, 'was again gratified by the appearance of Mrs Siddons on the stage'. She so queened it at the Theatre Royal that the Faculty of Advocates, Harry Erskine in the lead, were moved to present her with a silver salver.

Now, in high summer, Edinburgh would take its recreation out of doors. Advocates played bowls on the green of Heriot's Hospital. On two evenings each week, price of admission one shilling, the Comely Gardens behind Holyroodhouse opened for public entertainment; that is, to hear a group of violins sawing away in an old pigeon house. It was not thought quite the thing to go there.

Much more popular was the distinctively Scottish sport of golf. Said Topham, genuinely curious:

They play it with a small leathern ball, like a fives ball and a piece of wood, flat on one side, in the shape of a small bat, which is fastened at the end of a stick of three or four feet long at right angles to it. The art consists in striking the ball with this instrument, into a hole in the ground, in a smaller number of strokes than your adversary. This game has the superiority of cricket and tennis, in being less violent and dangerous; but in point of dexterity and amusement, by no means to be compared with them. However I am informed that some skill and nicety are necessary to strike the ball to the proposed distance and no further, and that in this there is a considerable difference in players. It requires no great exertion and strength, and all ranks and ages play at it. They instruct their children in it, as soon as they can run alone, and grey hairs boast their execution.

Then, in early August, for a whole week Edinburgh went to the races. For a betting man like Brodie it must have been galling not to take his usual place among the hundreds of carriages moving about the sands at Leith with a background of ships and boats and the distant hills of Fife, while hunters and heavy horses raced by the edge of the incoming tide. This year the Deacon had a different race to run. In his younger days he had joined the masonic lodge in the Canongate, where met the best of Edinburgh society. Long since he had deserted it for the burlesque freemasonry of the Cape. Did he now regret that this had been his path? Probably not. Life had now given William Brodie the leading role.

2
The Trial

In Edinburgh, judges walk to work. The August morning that began the trial of Deacon Brodie, saw the Lord Justice Clerk make his way to the Parliament House from his genteel grey home in George's Square, fully robed, full-wigged, his man in attendance, and on foot.

Lord Braxfield, old Braxie to young advocates, Robbie Macqueen to his cronies, had been Scotland's chief criminal judge since only a few months past, but for sheer force of intellect had no equal. An uncompromising Scot, he was deeply fond of his native tongue, Scottish ways and old Scots song, and despised his colleagues who stammered away in what they took to be polite English. In that century of privilege he was an astonishing man: his grandfather had been a gardener.

But gardener to an earl. The gardener's son got education, became factotum to the Earl of Selkirk for his properties in Lanarkshire and had married a daughter from the local gentry. It happened that the second Lord President Dundas had married into an estate down beside the ravine of the Clyde where it half-encircles the little upland burgh of Lanark. There in the long summer vacations he had taken a liking to Mr Macqueen's intelligent son, the brightest lad at the grammar school. The boy's broad Scots would be no barrier: it was the Lord President's tongue too.

With Dundas encouragement, young Macqueen progressed through the University of Edinburgh and qualification in the law, and was called to the Bar. In the flurry of cases about the forfeited estates of Jacobite gentlemen after the Forty-five he made his name as a Crown lawyer. Everyone respected

Robbie Macqueen. Even James Boswell, prickly as he was about rank and birth, thought highly of him. As the years went by, Dundas backing continued. In his mid-forties it took him to the Bench. The eldest son reared at his house down the Covenant Close near the Tron Kirk was Robert *Dundas* Macqueen. It gave him a Justiciary gown. Finally, in January 1788 it made him Lord Justice Clerk, Scotland's chief criminal judge. He lived for work, whist, deep drinking, fun (which the more prim of his contemporaries thought to be on the coarse side: *he* held it 'a glorious thing to talk nonsense') and the judicious enlargement of the estate of Braxfield by the banks of the Clyde where he had bird-nested as a boy.

Consider then Lord Braxfield this August morning as he came down the five steps outside his house at No. 13 George's Square and made his way along the still unpaved footpath past the houses of fellow judges and gentry. (No one in trade could live in this select *faubourg*.) He had the look of a black-smith, Henry Cockburn was to say forty years later, remembering the Scottish Bench of his youth. Another Whig like Cockburn, but one who did not have his knife in old Braxie was to put it differently. He was the kind of man Robert Burns might have become had he lived, said Ramsay of Ochtertyre; the same sturdy commonsense, the same fondness for fun, the same glow of quality. And when he painted him, Henry Raeburn saw twinkling eyes in a strong Scots face.

Braxfield was the man who beyond all doubt had displaced family prejudice and established the rule of reason on the Scottish Bench; he had done this by applying a mind as sharp as a cavalry sabre. The trouble was that it would fairly thwack anyone who got in his way, and sometimes his lady was at the receiving end. Were she to excuse the indifference of the dinner at No. 13 George's Square by praising the piety of the cook, she was slashed with 'I'd tak' a whure aff the streets gin she could bile a tattie.'* Himself avid for play and she no hand at whist, his lady could expect rough words when she trumped his ace. But his bark was worse than his bite. Somewhere there was a sentimental core to him. He had two rather beautiful daughters. Intellectually his sons were no great shakes, but they were doing well enough for themselves. And one suspects

---

* 'I'd take a tart from the streets if she could only cook the spuds.'

that despite the explosions his wife knew well enough how to
manage her husband.

Along the Potterow he walked, past the houses where (my
Lord would reflect) the poet Burns had been too friendly with
a married woman, then down to the Cowgate and up the long
flight of back stairs to the Parliament Close. A month past he
had dealt severely with an Edinburgh weaver. With others of
his kind the fellow had united against the employers for higher
wages. Worse still, they had got out of hand and mobbed their
masters. The weaver was a respectable enough family man
with a house over by the Calton Hill: a pity that there was
nothing for it but to have him flogged up and down the High
Street and banished from Scotland for seven years. The people
had to learn that the law was not to be kicked about like a
football.

As he *peched* to the top of the long stairs, his mind would be
recalled to the business in hand. That morning in the Parliament Close King Charles on his tunbellied horse looked over a
hubbub of people held back by soldiers from the Castle and
the halberds of the City Guard. There was work to be done.
Old Francis Brodie, Robbie Macqueen had known well.
It was a fearful thing that Lord Braxfield should have to hang
his son.

It was the Deacon the great crowd wanted to see. By now half
Edinburgh was claiming that for years they had suspected him
to be up to no good. Shopkeepers who had spoken to him at
the Cross about their need for a new lock, but had been slow
to conclude the bargain, would claim that it was something
more than lack of money that had made them draw back.
Mr James Cooper, jeweller on the South Bridge, smugly
recalled that he had broken his partnership with the unfortunate Bruce Brothers of the North Bridge because he could
not abide their friendship with Brodie. At the breakfast-table
that morning at No. 53 Princes Street, Mrs Harry Erskine, a
lady of great refinement, had observed to her husband that all
along she had disliked the man, however good the furniture
he made.

To their annoyance, that morning the crowd were to see
nothing of the Deacon. It was up to the Provost and to the

c

Bailies to make the trial arrangements. So, bayonets fixed, an escort from the Town Guard kept the mob away from the drawn blinds of the sedan chair which brought Brodie across the Parliament Close from the Tolbooth Prison. The dignity of the Town Council's black sheep must be preserved.

That morning the Deacon had put on a fashionable waistcoat and a dark blue coat, matching well the black satin of his breeches and his white silk stockings. So his thoughts would be in keeping with the smartness of his dress. At that moment he would be William Brodie, head of his profession, formerly a member of the Town Council, a power in the city who by a quirk of misfortune was to stand trial in the High Court. The leader of the Brodie gang would be forgotten. So too was the exile, pining for his two families from the wrong side of the blanket. Somewhere in his mind there would stick a memory of Sir Lewd who reeled from a Cape supper to gamble till dawn in the den down Fleshmarket Close, but this too would be pushed aside in the tingling excitement of the present, a feeling stronger than the thrill of winning at cards, headier even than crime. Today would see a keener match than was ever played at Michael Henderson's. We've got Harry Erskine to defend you, anxious friends had said when he came back to Edinburgh. '*Good*,' he had replied, '*so now we've got the best cock that ever fought.*' This was how life should be lived: coolness to match the daring.

Then as the crowd lowed away like so many cattle beasts outside the drawn blinds, he would bite his lip, and for the hundredth time reassess his chances. For sure, Harry Erskine would do his damnedest to make the jury see that he had fled the country for fear of what false witness that designing villain Brown might bear against him. The Crown was letting Brown and Ainslie turn King's evidence, but all Ilay Campbell had on his side were the accusations of these desperate men trying to save their own necks; and Harry had a trump card up his sleeve which would knock them out of that game. As for Smith, it was true that George, fool that he was, had made a full confession. Much good it had done him. He too was to stand in the dock. But the lawyers had persuaded George to retract, and no doubt Harry would find a way to persuade the jury that the confession had never been.

There were also, the Deacon would reflect uncomfortably,

the papers found in the big black trunk which had accompanied him to the Low Countries; and once again he would regret the shipboard letters he had written to Matthew Sheriff and Michael Henderson. But for these he would now be at his ease in New York, the wide Atlantic between him and my Lord Advocate. And yet an American exile would be a kind of death.

But, all might go well; and, as he stepped from the sedan on to the floor of the crowded courtroom, every seat taken, people crushed together like herring in boxes on the pier of Leith, he had a confident, alert look. And so, flanked by two soldiers of the City Guard he took his seat beside George Smith whose mean dress matched his hangdog look.

Now the court waited for the judges. As they watched counsel – black gowns and white wigs – busying themselves with their papers, the throng of Edinburgh bankers, shopkeepers, insurance brokers and such like from whom the jury was to be chosen might have reflected that not only was Erskine a Whig: *all* the defence counsel were Whig. Harry Erskine's junior was Alexander Wight. Like him he played Corelli beautifully at the concert off the Cowgate; but he had also been Solicitor-General in the Whig administration of five years past which for the space of a few months had made Erskine Lord-Advocate. By his side was Charles Hay, his feats more with the bottle than the violin, frequenting the Crochallan Club rather than St Cecilia's Hall, a jovial man with a big paunch and short legs, another well-known Whig. Counsel for Smith, John Clerk, was an untidy, unruly scion of a famous Midlothian family which had played a part in the nation's affairs long before the Dundases had emerged, and now had the name of being critical of Government.

There was much to be critical about. Only three weeks past in the Baxter's Hall there had been a crush of would-be reformers of the Scottish burghs. But they were powerless to do other than come to Edinburgh and protest. Only three months past at Westminster Henry Dundas had thrown out a bill to reform the burghal finances. 'It will be found', Great Hal had blandly informed the House, 'that the funds of the Scottish burghs are as well managed as those of any corporations in the Kingdom.' In private Dundas would admit that they were sinks of corruption and that 'it would be easier to reform Hell'. He might even concede in private that the state of the burghs

was a bar to the improvement of Scotland. But the management
of Parliament demanded the votes of the Scottish members;
and this meant that the town councils had to be bought, could
not be crossed.

The Dundas–Tory grip of Scotland had that summer been
brought home to Erskine and his friends by a confidential
survey they had had made for Mr Fox of the Scottish county
gentlemen, the two thousand who alone had the vote in the
shires. From county to county it had been depressingly uniform.
'Andrew Houston of Jordanhill has a large family whom he
must provide for', and so could not be expected to get on the
wrong side of Henry Dundas from whom all favours flowed.
Or there was the report on the gentlemen* of the Duke of
Argyll's country: 'The greatest part of them have very near
connections in the Army or Navy', it said. 'Many of them are
active enterprising men, desirous of promotion, and the Duke
it is thought would be in a very troublesome situation unless
he was acting with the Administration.' It was infuriating.
In the business of the General Assembly at St Giles in May,
Erskine had contrived to make a political debate even out of
the Church of Scotland's reply to King George's gracious
message. More than ever before, there was now political edge
between the Whig lawyers in the one camp and the Campbell
Lord-Advocate and his Solicitor-General – a Dundas of
course and nephew to Great Hal – in the other. Would it
show in the contest now beginning?

Like visitors from another age, if not another world, the
judges entered, bewigged, scarlet robed, the gold Justiciary
mace going in front. They took their chairs and Braxfield
bade the two prisoners stand while Josie Norris, the aged
Clerk of Court, read the indictment:

WILLIAM BRODIE, sometime wright and cabinet-maker in Edinburgh, and GEORGE SMITH, sometime grocer there, both prisoners
in the Tolbooth of Edinburgh, you are indicted and accused at the
instance of Ilay Campbell, Esquire, his Majesty's Advocate, for his
Majesty's interest: THAT ALBEIT, by the laws of this, and of every

* Campbells (pronounced Ca'mels) to a man; said to be more of them
than in all the deserts of Arabia (eighteenth-century joke).

other well governed realm, THEFT, more especially when attended
with house-breaking, and when committed by breaking into a house
used or kept as an Excise Office, or other public office, under cloud
of night, and from thence abstracting and stealing money, is a
crime of a heinous nature and severaly punishable. YET TRUE IT
IS AND OF VERITY, that you, the said William Brodie, and George
Smith, are both, and each, or one or other of you guilty actors in
art and part of the same crime . . .

The attention of the waiting burgesses would stray as they
reflected on their Lordships of the Bench. Edinburgh being
what it was, they would know all about them. Hailes, a finicky
scholar, something of a dry old stick, loving his country house
near Musselburgh, sweetmeats and sweet wines, his weak voice
and acquired English forever drawing the contempt of Braxfield. Swinton, mindful always that he was a Swinton of
Swinton but also a border gentleman with a big family and
sound sense; he had successfully agitated for the laying of a
gravel path round the Meadows, and Edinburgh always
prizes most this sort of achievement. Stonefield, a Campbell
laird like the Lord-Advocate, the interests of Argyll ever upper-
most in his mind; said to be disagreeable to his family, the
new house in George's Square no haven of contentment when
he was in liquor. Eskgrove – but more than a sentence would
be needed to encompass Lord Eskgrove.

He had the face of a clown, a scurfy blue when it was not a
scurfy red. He had a big nose and a prodigious chin which,
said Henry Cockburn, moved like the jaw of a Dutch toy;
and he hirpled rather than walked, his elbows going all the
time like fins. He mumbled rather than spoke, pronouncing
words by syllables, the accent going on the last; and the
terminal g was always given special treatment. King James was
Kingge Jam-es. He was long-winded beyond all endurance.
When he was presiding judge, the charge to the wretched
jurors *standing* in their box would go on for hours. But he was
learned in the law, and he could on occasion be the Lord
Justice Clerk's superior in humanity. The Calton weaver
whom Braxfield had had whipped through the streets would
have been spared this had 'Esky' had his way.

Rich though they were by Edinburgh standards, the judges
would not be remote figures. Just as everyone accepted that
Lord Gardenstone kept a pig for a pet and that Lord

Monboddo was mad keen for exercise, trudging to court even through an Edinburgh downpour (but sending on his wig by sedan chair), so they would accept Eskgrove's leering eye for the ladies and Braxfield's thunder.

Whatever their eccentricities, the judges would be looked on with respect. They and their colleagues had raised Scots law to a height from which the confusion of the English courts could be regarded with a sturdy sense of superiority. Here in Scotland a prisoner had counsel to help him; in England a wretch on trial for a felony had to stand in court unaided. Here reason ruled. It was a far cry to the days when considerations of family had equal claim to those of law. Here was the Enlightenment at work: and it was less than forty years since the Lord-President of the day had believed in witches.

... You, the said William Brodie and George Smith, did, by means of false keys or other instruments, wickedly and feloniously break into the house in which the General Excise Office for Scotland was then kept, in Chessel's buildings, on the south side of Canongate of Edinburgh, within the royalty or liberties of the city of Edinburgh, and did thence feloniously abstract and steal money ...

The indictment went on, itemizing the trunk which had accompanied Brodie to Holland, the tools used for the break-in and the pair of pistols so nearly used on little Mr Bonar that night in Chessel's Court six months past.

... ALL WHICH, or part thereof, being found proven by the verdict of an assize before the Lord Justice Clerk, Lord Justice General and Lords Commissioners of Judiciary. you, the said William Brodie and George Smith OUGHT to be punished with the pains of law, to deter others from committing the like crimes in all times coming.

The Lord Justice Clerk turned to the prisoners (in Scots law the *pannels*: in Braxfield's accent the *paynnels*)

'Are ye guilty o' the crime there charged or no' guilty?'

'Ma' Lord, ah'm no guilty,' said Brodie, as if he meant it.

'Not guilty, my Lord,' mumbled Smith.

Braxfield then asked counsel for the *paynnels* if they had any objection to the indictment. None, said Mr Hay, for Brodie; there is an alibi.

'My Lords,' Erskine intervened, correct English, Scots delivery, 'we undertake to prove that, before eight o'clock of that night in which the Excise Office is said to have been broken into, Mr Brodie went to the house of Janet Watt, a person residing in Libberton's Wynd with whom he had a peculiar connection, and that he remained in that house from the said hour until about nine o'clock the next morning.'

The Lord Justice Clerk would know that the 'peculiar connection' was carnal, Janet Watt no better than she should be.

Smith rests his defence on a denial of the charge, said his counsel, young Mr Clerk. He has no alibi.

Then Braxfield picked the jury out of the forty-five citizens of Edinburgh in waiting. They were given pen, ink, paper and copies of the indictment, and were empanelled. Of the chosen fifteen six were bankers; four merchants; James Donaldson then making a fortune for himself printing pirated editions of English authors thanks to the less restrictive Scottish law of copyright; and William Creech. That Creech was there by the mere chance of selection may be doubted. The town's foremost publisher already foresaw in print and bound octavo, *An Account of the Trial of William Brodie by William Creech, one of the Jury*, to be on sale in the shop in the Luckenbooths within the week. It should do even better than the *Poems chiefly in the Scottish dialect* by Mr Burns.

This ambition to give the public a word by word record of the coming battle of giants was shared by another of the watching faces in the crowded courtroom. This was Mr Aeneas Morison, an Edinburgh Writer to the Signet whom the Court had appointed as agent for the destitute Smith. And young Mr Morison was agog with excitement. Like his friend John Clerk, this was his first big case.

Now at the outset, before the trial was properly begun, there was a skirmish for position. That Brodie had unwisely consorted with criminals, Erskine was prepared to concede. He could do little else: all Edinburgh knew about the goings on in Clark's Tavern. But he could claim that this was no more than the Deacon's addiction to gaming. What would be difficult to explain away would be anything which implied an admission of guilt on the Deacon's part. Some means had to be found to cast doubt on those incriminating but unsigned papers found in Brodie's trunk. The indictment had listed these papers along with a watch and other objects found in the trunk, and they would try to show that each and all belonged to Brodie.

If it was his watch, it was his trunk; if it was his trunk, the unsigned papers were Brodie's. Let doubt be cast on the ownership of the trunk, and the harm the papers might do him would vanish. This, at any rate was the tactics the defence would employ, as Harry Erskine had explained to Aeneas Morison.

So in very correct English:

MR WIGHT: I attend your Lordships on the part of Mr Brodie, and although there does not appear upon the face of the indictment any sufficient ground for an objection to the relevancy of it, yet there are some particulars of which I consider it my duty to take notice. The law of this country has been very careful to give unhappy men in the situation of the prisoners every opportunity of preparing for their trials. The present indictment is laid in the most vague and general manner I have ever seen. Here there are certain letters and declarations founded on, and other articles, such as a gold watch with a chain, and seal, and key, a chest or trunk containing various articles. These are mentioned in so vague a manner as not to distinguish them from other articles of the same kind, consequently in such a manner as not to give the pannels proper opportunity of preparing for their defence. This is the more inexcusable that all of these articles admitted of a more accurate description.

THE LORD JUSTICE CLERK: Mr Wight, thae objections are oot o' place. They ocht tae be stated when the articles you mention come tae be produced by the prosecutor.

But there had even been confusion in the Justiciary Office about the Deacon's trunk, said Wight. Only a few days past, asked to make available the various articles mentioned in the indictment for inspection by the Defence, the Crown authorities had produced the wrong trunk.

The Defence were making a mountain out of a molehill, replied Solicitor-General Dundas, a small pleasant spry man of no great ability. Out of common humanity the Deacon's trunk had been returned to him to hold his belongings while he was in the Tolbooth prison. Nor, intervened Ilay Campbell, the Highland intonation in his voice, had the Defence's contention a leg to stand on.

It may be necessary to prove that certain letters were found in the chest, and to whom the chest belonged; it is no matter of what form the chest is, and not of the smallest consequence whether it is identified or not. If every nail of a trunk or every trinket of a watch, or other articles which it might be necessary to found upon in trials of this kind, were to be so particularly described as Mr Wight has contended for, it would swell indictments to a very inconvenient and unnecessary length.

Harry Erskine could not let it go at that. When he visited the Parliament House two summers past, Burns had caught the look of the Dean of Faculty at moments like this as the Lord-Advocate and he rubbed each other the wrong way. First the arm extended, emphasizing each well-arranged point; then the words coming like wind-driven hail while Ilay Campbell watched the gathering storm 'wi' ruefu' e'e'. So now Erskine began in a homely, half-humorous style.

Suppose, for instance, that a person breaks into a house and leaves his hat behind him; nothing could establish his guilt more clearly than to prove that this hat was his. Would it be enough to say that a hat was to be produced in evidence, without specifying where it was found, or any circumstances attending it, so as to give the accused an opportunity of proving that it belonged to another, and not to him?

Then, inexorably to the peroration, raising the standard of principle above the skirmish:

My Lords, it is our good fortune to live under a mild Government; to live in days when there is no danger to be apprehended from the conduct of the public prosecutor. But worse times may arrive, and it is for your Lordships to reflect upon what use might then be made of the present practice if your Lordships were to allow it to be now introduced. The dearest rights of mankind might be endangered and at the mercy of corrupt men, and no one could say how fatal the consequences might be.

He was playing to young Edinburgh in the gallery.

Braxfield turned to his colleagues. 'Whit's your *opeenion?*' he asked, his voice no doubt conveying that he would not think much of anything they had to say. Knowing that the Lord Justice Clerk looked on Hailes as an old sweetie-wife, perhaps Erskine winced when he heard Hailes give it as his careful view that the objection to the admissibility of the Deacon's travelling trunk should be sustained.

Then it was Eskgrove's turn, the great jaw moving as if by clockwork, the words curiously declaimed by syllables. 'My

Laards,' he said 'I am not dis-pos-ed to a-bridge in the small-est de-gree the sec-ur-ity of the sub-jects of this count-ry.' But his opinion was for repelling the objection. So was Stonefield's. So was Swinton's.

The Lord Justice Clerk had been listening to all this twaddle in a fidget of impatience. He did not so much repel the objection. He scythed it away.

'A'hm ane o' thae folk wha are aye for ge'in fair play tae paynnels, an' ahl' never allow ony advantage to be taken o' them. But, jist the same, ah'm for ge'in fair play tae *evidence*.'

The law, he said, was crystal-clear. Everyone had over-looked 'Act one-hunner an' fifty three' of the Eleventh Parlia-ment of King James VI. It made a nonsense of the Dean of Faculty's objection.

That was an end of the matter, except that John Clerk rose to object.

'Whit!' thundered Braxfield. 'Aifter the Court hae gien their opeenions, it's no decent of you tae propose tae say onything. Onyway,' he sneered at the young advocate on this his first appearance in the High Court of Justiciary, 'the prisoners are in nae danger o' sufferin' anything by *your* no bein' allowed tae supply the defects o' the Dean o' Faculty.'

'My Lord, the Dean of Faculty has nae authority to plead for ma' client,' said Clerk bravely. Like Braxfield he too stuck to broad Scots.

But Erskine was quickly to his feet to intervene. An objection was put on record, and left at that.

So the trial proper began; Aeneas Morison had never seen anything like it.

As noon came near, the bells under the ancient Gothic crown of St Giles played away, their jangle coming through the stone walls of the Parliament House while the Lord Justice Clerk laid down the law and the jurymen thought of the midday dram that would not be theirs. On this, as on every weekday, gentlemen gathered at noon in the handsome panelled room of Douglas's Tavern in Anchor Close, down Libberton's Wynd in the darkened snugness of Johnnie Dowie's, and at a score of other drinking howffs for their meridian;* small claret at

* Meridian: midday refreshment.

tenpence the bottle, Bell's beer, and Younger's Edinburgh ale.
For Mr Creech and his fellow jurors there was no such
entertainment. But in a little while they would have the
privilege of watching the Bench refresh themselves. Henry
Cockburn remembered how it was at these moments. First,
black bottles of strong port set down on the bench with glasses,
carafes of water, tumblers and biscuits. Then an interval while
the refreshment was allowed to stand untouched. Next, some
water poured into a tumbler and quietly sipped, 'as if merely
to sustain nature'; and after this a little wine with water. Then
'at last patience could endure no longer, and a full bumper of
the pure black element was tossed over; after which the thing
went on regularly, and there was a comfortable munching and
quaffing to the great envy of the parched throats in the gallery'.

In their toping the Bench were only keeping up with the
Bar. It was not unknown for learned counsel to come to Court
straight from the nightlong carouse. 'Gentlemen,' said Braxfield on one occasion to the opposing advocates, one of whom
was Charles Hay, 'ye maun jist pack up yer papers and gang
hame. The tane o' ye's riftin' punch. The tither's belchin'
claret. There'll be nae guid got oot o' ye the day.'

James Wolfe Murray, godson to the hero of Quebec, now took
the prosecution witnesses through their evidence. In this
respect the criminal law of Scotland was – is – so markedly
superior to the arrangements which obtain south of the Tweed.
No opening barrage from prosecuting counsel: fact by fact the
careful building-up of the case from the evidence led.

Each witness was brought before the Clerk of Justiciary and
the defence given an opportunity formally to object to him.
Then the Lord Justice Clerk had the witness, right hand raised,
repeat the solemn oath 'as I shall answer to God on the Great
Day of Judgment'. The witness was asked if anyone had told
him what to say, and if he had any ill-will against the prisoner.
Then the examination began.

In quick succession appeared Mr Scott, the Edinburgh
Procurator-Fiscal; Mr Langlands, the London solicitor who
had been engaged by the Lord-Advocate in the quest for the
fugitive Deacon, and now identified Brodie's trunk and the
bundle of papers it had held; and John Geddes, the Mid

Calder tobacconist who described Brodie's voyage from the
Thames on the *Endeavour* of Carron.

There was little that Erskine could do to cover the nakedness
of the fact that the Deacon had fled to the Low Countries as if
indeed he were a criminal on the run. But some fun could be
had at the expense of the village tobacconist who had behaved
shabbily all round, neither delivering the letters Brodie had
entrusted to him, nor promptly handing them over to the
Sheriff of Edinburgh. Erskine's country house at Almondell
was near to Mid Calder. Perhaps the village tobacconist kept
poor snuff.

THE DEAN OF FACULTY – You have told us that you went ashore
   when you arrived in Flushing. Pray, sir, did you make any
   purchases there?
GEDDES – None, except a piece or twa' o' nankeen for breeches to
   masel.
THE DEAN OF FACULTY – You will remember, sir, that you are
   upon your great oath, and that it is your duty to tell the whole
   truth. Did you purchase no lace, sir, when you was at Flushing?
GEDDES – A few yairds.
THE DEAN OF FACULTY – Why, then, did you say that you pur-
   chased nothing except the nankeen?
GEDDES – It was ma' wife and no me that bocht it.
THE DEAN OF FACULTY – Did you offer the lace for sale?
GEDDES – No, there's pairt o' it aboot a cloak ma' wife has wi' her
   here.
THE DEAN OF FACULTY – And what became of the rest of it?
   Remember, sir, you are upon your great oath.
GEDDES – That was it a', except a few yairds ah sell't at Bathgate
   for twenty-twa shillin'.
THE DEAN OF FACULTY – Did you not say even now that you had
   offered none of it for sale?
GEDDES (very uncomfortable) – I said I offered nane o' it for sale
   here in Enbru.
THE DEAN OF FACULTY – Pray, sir, when did you open these
   letters you have told us of? Was it before or after you came to
   Leith?
GEDDES – It was aifter.
THE DEAN OF FACULTY – You told us, sir, that upon reading the
   newspapers you discovered that Dixon and Brodie were one and
   the same person. How long was that after your arrival?
GEDDES – Three weeks.
THE DEAN OF FACULTY – And pray, sir, what was the reason that

'in all that time you did not deliver these letters to the persons to whom they were directed?

GEDDES – I didna remember that I had sic letters when I was in Edinburgh masel', and aifterwards I wished ma brother-in-law tae deliver them.

THE DEAN OF FACULTY – Did you open the letters?

GEDDES – Ah did.

THE DEAN OF FACULTY – And what was your reason for doing so?

GEDDES – Ah opened them and delivered them tae the Sheriff for the guid o' ma' country.

THE DEAN OF FACULTY – And would it not have been as much for the good of the country to have delivered them without opening them?

GEDDES – Ah jist opened them, and that's a'. Ah can gie nae ither reason.

Mrs Margaret Geddes was then called to confirm her husband's story. 'Did you or your husband make any purchases while in Flushing?' asked Erskine.

Braxfield would stand no more nonsense. 'Margaret,' he interrupted, 'if you or your husband bocht ony contraband goods when ye wis at Flushing, you'll tell the Court, and you hae naething tae fear.'

Reading the storm warnings aright, Harry Erskine gave up the chase.

The foreman from Brodie's yard spoke of the Sunday morning in March when his master had left town while the city was at church. He would not meet the Lord-Advocate's purpose by saying that the papers in the trunk were in Brodie's hand. But the City Chamberlain said he thought they were, explaining that he knew the hand from the many bills rendered for Council locks fitted and doors altered by the Deacon of the Wrights over the years.

The porter and the housekeeper at Chessel's Court told how they found that the Excise Office had been robbed. The loss of money which had been so little and could have been so much was detailed by the Office's accountant. Tiny Mr Bonar spoke of the man in the black coat and a great hurry whom he had disturbed that dark March evening.

There was nothing damaging to Brodie in this. Mr Bonar would certainly know the Deacon but he had not identified him. Nor was there anything particularly troublesome in the evidence by a farm servant from Duddingston, the village nestled under the far side of Arthur's Seat, which linked Smith with the theft of the coulter from his plough, the implement which had prised open the doors at Chessel's Court. Smith's maidservant spoke of the evening of the crime in her master's house above the Cowgate shop. Brodie had been there in an old-fashioned black coat, she said. She had taken notice of this; though she had at other times seen him in black clothes, 'they were always of a newer fashion'. Later that night she saw him again but now he had on his fine white suit. Curious as an Edinburgh serving lass would be, 'I expressed my surprise to my mistress that Mr Brodie should wear such a strange dress when he came in the first time in his old black clothes, and she answered that it was his frolic.' (So Aeneas Morison, striving for polite English, took down what the servant-lass said. It is unlikely that these were her words to the Court; still less likely that this was what passed between her and her mistress that afternoon. The reality would more probably be 'Whit wey's the Deacon a' dressed up like a dish o' fish when he had the duds o' an auld gangrel body on his back, four hours syne?')

But again, none of this was particularly harmful to Brodie. Erskine quickly had it out of the girl that the Deacon had often played at cards with the Cowgate grocer, and that there was nothing unusual in them supping together on Bell's beer and fresh herring. Then the Defence had a small success in preventing the Prosecution calling Smith's wife on account of a misnomer.

She was a petite, attractive Englishwoman, and as big a villain as her husband in that it was she who maintained the link with Mr Tasker alias Murray of Chesterfield, the Anglo-Scottish fence. On entering the Court she rushed to her husband in the dock and kissed him warmly before the officers of the Court could get to her. As they pulled her away, Smith held out his manacled hands to her, entreating her to answer no questions. 'Whit, my Lords,' said Clerk, 'are ye cruelly gaun tae allow this man's wife tae be called against her ain husband, here strugglin' in the presence o' yer Lordships for his life?'

Cheers from the overflowing public benches. But the judges ruled that she could be an evidence against the Deacon, and turned a deaf ear to the obvious plea that evidence against the one must tell agaist the other.

Erskine bided his time; he could afford to, for the Defence had been busy; and when Braxfield had administered the oath to the weeping witness he said blandly, 'Madam, will you please to speak up and tell me your maiden name.'

'My name, sir,' she replied between sobs, 'is Mary Hubbert.'

'Quite so,' said Erskine, 'now will you please to write it down.'

'Now, my Lords,' said Erskine, holding up the list of witnesses, 'there is no such witness in the indictment. We have, as your Lordships may see there' (holding up what the grocer's wife had written) 'a "Mary *Hubbert*" but' (holding up his copy of the indictment) 'we have no Mary *Hibutt*. The difference between these names is as great as if your Lordships were to call me Henry Friskin.' And in support of what he said, he produced the extract of her birth from an English parish register obtained, as it must have been, at no small trouble and expense.

Perhaps the strong black port was at work, for Hailes the historian now went off on a digression about the several variations in the name of Hobart, 'the name of a very respectable family of Buckinghamshire'. Eskgrove began what had all the appearance of a long dissertation on the difference between Scotch practice which gives the maiden name, and the English which does not. It was too much for Ilay Campbell: he interrupted his Lordship to ask that they pass forthwith to the next witness. Mistress Smith curtsied and withdrew. This round to Erskine.

An Edinburgh ironmonger spoke of a saw he had sold to Brodie which could have been used to burst locks; but then he recalled that the Deacon had bought the saw to cut off the natural spurs of his fighting cocks. Middleton the Sheriff's man described the unearthing of the caches where the keys and crowbars were hid. Other Sheriff's officers told of the search they had made of the big house off Brodie's Close and in the cabinet-maker's yard above the Cowgate where were found pistols and a dark lanthorn. George Williamson gave the court rather more detail than they wished of his quest for Brodie from Dunbar, to Newcastle, to York, to London, to Deal in Kent, and then to London again to bring him back to Edinburgh.

'The next witness,' said the Solicitor-General, 'is Andrew Ainslie.'

Erskine rose to speak, and Aeneas Morison gripped his pen the tighter. At the last consultation, Harry Erskine had said that 'all the fire of the artillery' must be turned on Ainslie and Brown, the two who had turned King's evidence. Now the crisis was at hand. And the Deacon would know it too; he likewise would be pulsing with the thrill of the moment.

All three of the Brodie gang had confessed. But Ainslie, the shoemaker, had been late in offering to give evidence for the Crown, and so it could be said that he was only swimming with the tide. Brown was an English convict on the run. Could the Court be moved to rule either inadmissible, the Crown might be unable to marshal enough of a case to hang Brodie. These would be the thoughts in Erskine's mind as he rose to challenge Ainslie's right to be a witness.

THE DEAN OF FACULTY – My Lords, I contend that this witness is inadmissible. When this witness was apprehended and committed to prison, in the month of March last, to stand trial for this crime, he never charged Mr Brodie as having been in any measure accessory thereto. On Ainslie's first examination he positively affirmed that Mr Brodie had no sort of accession to the crime of which he is now accused, or was concerned in any other bad action whatever to his knowledge, unless playing at cards and dice should be reckoned such; and in the different declarations which he made before the Sheriff he still persisted in denying that my client had any concern in this robbery. But after Mr Brodie was apprehended and brought from Holland, Ainslie was again brought before the Sheriff, when he was informed that either he himself must be hanged or he must accuse Mr Brodie.

I mean to say nothing against the conduct of the Sheriff, which may have been very proper. With the motives which may have influenced a public officer to a particular line of conduct I have nothing to do. But I state it as an insuperable bar to the admissibility of this witness, that hopes were suggested to him of saving his own life by criminating my client. And I offer to prove, by the evidence of the Sheriff of Edinburgh himself, that a bargain of this nature was made with Ainslie, and that it was not till then he was prevailed upon to say that Mr Brodie had any concern in this crime. No man could withstand such a temptation, and it is impossible that the Court can receive the testimony of a witness in such circumstances.

Kay's caricature 'The first meeting of Deacon Brodie and George Smith'. Also shown are the Deacon's gamecock and Smith's Labrador.

Thus we poor Cocks, exert our skill & Brav'ry
For idle Gulls, and Kites that trade in Knav'ry

Henderson's cockpit in the Grassmarket as Kay saw it. The Deacon's
is the face with the scar at the right-hand edge of the drawing.

Creech's bookshop in the Luckenbooths beside the High Church (St Giles).

Eliphinstone Drawings

Above: Parliament House, the Parliament Close and King Charles II on horseback

Below: The High Street and the Tron Kirk before the building of the South Bridge.

Kay caricatures

Top left : Lord Eskgrove
Top right : Lord Stonefield
Below : Lord Hailes

An array of advocates depicted by Kay. John Clerk (spectacles on his brow) is second on the right-hand file. Below him is Henry Erskine.

Kay caricatures
Left: Ilay Campbell, the Lord Advocate
Right: Henry Dundas tells his nephew the Solicitor-General what to do.

The hanging of Brodie and Smith 1st October 1788 – a contemporary drawing.

Raeburn portraits

Top left: John Clerk
Top right: Henry Erskine
Bottom Left: Lord Braxfield
Bottom right: William Creech

In his dull voice the Lord-Advocate gave a reply which his *unfriends* would say was worthy of a Ca'mell. He answered at some length points Erskine had not made; said it was not to be believed that the Sheriff would strike a bargain with a man in Ainslie's position; and then capped it by saying that such a bargain even if made would not bind the Lord-Advocate.

THE DEAN OF FACULTY – My Lords, I offer to prove my assertion.

THE LORD JUSTICE CLERK – Dean of Faculty, dae ya say that ma' Lord Advocate has made a corrupt bargain wi' the witness tae accuse Mr Brodie upon condition o' receiving a pardon?

DEAN OF FACULTY – No, my Lord. But I repeat my offer to prove a bargain to that purpose with the Sheriff.

But Erskine was to be given no chance to do so. First Hailes bumbled on about the wrong-headedness of Sir George Mackenzie when that great authority of the previous century wrote on the inadmissibility of accomplices. Eskgrove argued somewhat naïvely that even if there had been a bargain, Ainslie was under no constraint since he could not now be charged for his part in the Chessel's Court break-in. Stonefield, in character, had nothing to say. Swinton was for Ainslie's admissibility. Then Braxfield had the last word.

THE LORD JUSTICE CLERK – My Lords, were sic an objection as this tae be sustained we would find verra few instances where a crime sic as this o' an occult and secret nature, could be broucht tae licht. What is said by the Dean of Faculty aboot a supposed bargain betwixt the Sheriff o' Edinburgh and Ainslie is by nae means sic an objection as affects his admissibeelity. The Sheriff is only an inferior officer, and had nae power tae enter into ony sic transaction. It's therefore no eneuch tae say that offers were made him by the Sheriff, whatever they were.

Ainslie was to testify. How the Sheriff of Edinburgh had bought his witness was to be glossed over.

Then Braxfield put the fear of God into the quivering soul of the Edinburgh cobbler.

THE LORD JUSTICE CLERK – Andra Ainslie, ye will remember that by the great oath ye hae sworn ye are bound tae tell the truth, and if ye say onything tae the prejudice of the prisoners which is no true, or if ye conceal ony part o' the truth ye wull be guilty o' the crime o' perjury, an' liable tae be tried and punished for it, and ye wull likewise commit a heinous sin in the sicht o' Goad and thereby endanger the eternal salvation of your ain soul.

For Ilay Campbell, Ainslie was a good witness. The Brodie gang, he said, had long planned the Excise Office job; and over a period Brown and he had kept an evening watch on Chessel's Court. So doing, they had seen that the big door to the Excise Office was locked at eight every evening and that the two night watchmen did not come on duty until ten. He confirmed that the coulter they used to burst open doors and desks in the Excise Office they had 'found' in a field near Duddingston. On Wednesday the 5th of March, which they had fixed as the night for the break-in, Brown and he had gone at dusk to the parkland under the Salisbury Craigs to fetch the coulter to Smith's house above the Cowgate shop. There Brodie joined them, his smart white great coat over the black suit he was to wear at the break-in.

As to the happenings in Chessel's Court, Ainslie again went over the bungled sequence of events, as he had described them to the Sheriff of Edinburgh, and told – doubtless to the horror of Mr Bonar's brother in the jury – how the diminutive Deputy-Solicitor of Excise had narrowly escaped being pistolled by the Brodie gang when he disturbed them at work. But for the Deacon losing his nerve and running away, he would have been a dead man.

When the Brodie gang reassembled by ones and twos at George Smith's house, there was anger and recrimination, said Ainslie. Brodie tried to laugh it off, but all knew that he had been found wanting, taking to his heels when coolness and daring were needed. They had shared out the miserable haul, Brown and Ainslie had then gone to a tavern in the New Town, and the black-suited figure with his father's old wig for disguise had become again the debonair Deacon.

Erskine did not trouble himself to put Ainslie under the harrow. All that mattered now was to have Brown, the second King's evidence, ruled inadmissible as a witness. Unsupported, Ainslie's evidence could not hang his client; the Defence could be confident should that have to stand alone.

From the quaint Tolbooth of the Canongate where he and Ainslie had been kept well away from the Deacon and his machinations, Brown had been marched that morning by the City Guard. Now he was called into the courtroom. Alexander Wight rose, supremely confident that a piece of paper he held in his hand would be a disabling broadside against the Crown, toppling masts and rigging to the deck. By exercise of the royal prerogative the Crown could legitimately overlook Brown's part in the Excise Office raid in order to secure his evidence against the Deacon. But he was sure they could not overlook a previous conviction; and the Defence had got from England written proof of Brown's criminal record.

MR WIGHT – My Lords, before this witness is called in, I have to object to his being received as a witness upon grounds which, I imagine, are insuperable.

This man, My Lords, was convicted at the General Quarter Sessions for the County of Middlesex, by the verdict of a jury, of stealing twenty-one guineas and fourteen doubloons, in consequence of which he was adjudged to be transported beyond the seas for the term of seven years, in April 1784, and this is instantly instructed by a copy of the said conviction, under the hand of the proper officer, now produced. And further, the witness, under the name of John Brown, was banished by the Justices of Peace for Stirlingshire from that county in September 1787, upon his confessing a theft committed at Falkirk, as appears from a certified copy of the said sentence under the hand of the Clerk of the Peace of the said shire.

I shall not take up your Lordships' time in proving that a man thus infamous is altogether inadmissible as a witness in any cause, especially where life is concerned, and I have no doubt that your Lordships will sustain the objection.

But Solicitor-General Dundas was also smiling.

THE SOLICITOR-GENERAL – My Lords, in answer to this objection, I here produce His Majesty's most gracious pardon in behalf of this witness, under the Great Seal of England, dated 28th July last, which, by the law of England, renders the witness habile and testable.

This made the public benches buzz like a wasp's nest. All of a sudden, as Aeneas Morison was to remember, Erskine lost his look of brisk geniality: he had not reckoned that the Crown would have the effrontery to stretch the royal pardon to cover a previous transportation offence. The Stirlingshire conviction was a small matter, and being a sentence imposed by a local court might not count. But a sentence of transportation by an Old Bailey judge – a sentence Brown had skipped – *must* be a bar to his appearing in Court. Looking at the box where the

Deacon was seated, flanked by two of the City Guard, Morison thought he saw him suddenly look faint.

However, Alexander Wight was quick to riposte.

MR WIGHT – The production of this pardon, my Lords, will by no means answer the objection which I have stated. The infamy attending the commission of the crimes of which Brown has been convicted is not, cannot be, done away by the King's pardon. He still remains a man unworthy of credit, in whom the gentlemen of the jury can place no confidence. His situation, in short, is just the same as it was before the granting of the pardon, unless that the pardon saves him from the punishment awarded against his crimes. This doctrine is delivered by Sir George Mackenzie in very strong terms, and it is the doctrine of commonsense.

Ilay Campbell made a shifty reply. Was the 'John Brown from Ireland' whom the Stirlingshire justices had banished the same man? Even if he were, his confession of guilt to this minor court for minor offences was unnecessary; it would have been enough for him simply to have accepted banishment from the county and kept his mouth shut. As to the General Excise Office break-in, Brown had never been charged with this crime, so the objection to Ainslie could not be levelled against him.

Laying aside these evasions, the Government's chief law officer then spoke frankly to the Court in terms which Mr Creech and his fellow shopkeepers of the jury would understand.

Many daring robberies have been committed in this city, and, in spite of the utmost vigilance of the police, no discovery could be made of the perpetrators. At length, upon the Friday after the robbery of the Excise Office, Brown went to Mr Middleton and told him such circumstances as led to a discovery. From this, my Lords, I am bound to suppose that he had repented of what he had done, and I conceived it to be my duty not to prosecute him, but, on the contrary, to make use of his evidence as a means of discovery of the rest of his accomplices. After this, my Lords, it was found that he had been convicted at the Old Bailey. I then applied for advice to those whom I thought were best enabled to assist me concerning the law of England on this subject, and I learned that the proper method to be followed was to apply for a pardon. I applied for a pardon and accordingly obtained it.

Then, a Campbell once more, he went back on his tracks.

The pardon he had obtained for Brown was unnecessary because the Old Bailey sentence of 1784 from which he had fled was a foreign sentence; and 'my Lord Kames declares himself to be clearly of the opinion that no weight whatever is attached to a foreign decree'. (Kames who had died only four years past was pre-eminent amongst his fellow judges. They thought the world of him: *he* called them 'auld bitches'.)

Even if this were not so, said Ilay Campbell in conclusion, 'His Majesty's most gracious pardon which I hold in my hand puts an end to all objections at once. A pardon from the King takes away the effects of any former sentence, and makes the person pardoned precisely the same person he was before the sentence was pronounced against him.'

There it was. More than the Deacon's guilt was now on trial. What was now at issue was the intrusion into Scotland of the overriding power which the Crown enjoyed in England. The law of England held that the King's prerogative could so expunge the misdeeds of even the blackest villain that he could bring down others by his bartered evidence for the Crown: conviction by a Scottish jury debarred altogether any such future appearance as a Crown witness. The English practice, my Lord-Advocate would say, was a safeguard against crime of an occult nature. Erskine's reply would be that it was a power which could put the individual at the mercy of tyrannical authority, an attack on the ancient liberties of Scotland.

In the heat of that August afternoon and the crowded courtroom Erskine's fears for the future would be sharpened by the knowledge of the Prosecution's game he could not bring into play. Ilay Campbell and Solicitor-General Dundas would concede – they could do none other – that a previous conviction by this High Court of Justiciary would make Brown inadmissible. Even were he pardoned by the King, the fact of a Scottish conviction of this gravity would mean that he could not give evidence for the Crown against his fellows. What Prosecution, Defence and the Bench all knew was that only three weeks past, Brown should have stood trial in this same court for violent crime. The Irishman was a murderer as well as a thief.

It was in March that Brown had told the Sheriff the lurid story of the Brodie gang; and since he was turning King's evidence he was not arrested. But in the month of May he was arrested and consigned to the Tolbooth; for the authorities had by then learned of his hand in a murder the previous winter.

The story was sordid. One night the previous November, George White, the elderly Inspector of Hides at the Flesh-market, drunk and diverting on his way home to the bawdy-house in Halkerston's Wynd, had come to blows with its keeper. The sluts of the establishment had joined with their patron in the battle, and the errant inspector had gone home nursing his wrath as well as his bruises. He then enlisted Brown, this choleric Irishman, and together they went back to the brothel. This time the innkeeper was left on the floor, his head smashed with blows from a bottle and a heavy candlestick.

On the 5th of August, in this same courtroom, Solicitor-General Dundas prosecuting, my Lord Justice Clerk presiding, George White on his own had stood trial for murder. Brown was named in the indictment but was not in court. White was found guilty of culpable homicide and given only a few months' imprisonment and a fine; a sentence which is perhaps not to be explained except on the supposition that the wielder of the brass candlestick and broken bottle was John Brown, already designated for a royal pardon for all his crimes.*

Erskine had a grand theme, and he made the most of it. He too spoke in terms which the bankers and businessmen of the jury would quickly grasp.

His Majesty's pardon, it is said – this pardon now produced to your Lordships, and obtained for the sole purpose of endeavouring to enable this man to be a witness – has now placed him in the same situation as if he had never been condemned.

My Lords, I have heard it said that the King could make a peer, but that he could not make a gentleman. I am sure that he cannot make a rogue an honest man. This pardon, therefore, at the utmost can only avert the punishment which follows from the sentence. It cannot remove the guilt of this man, though it may save his life. Can it, indeed, my Lords, be supposed that this amiable prerogative, lodged in the hands of the King for the wisest of purposes, and to be exerted by him as the father of his people, should have the effect to let loose persons upon society, as honest, respectable men, men who may be witnesses, who may be jurymen, and may decide upon your lives or my life tomorrow, although these very persons were yester-day in the eye of the law and the eye of reason held as hardened

* See Appendix 1.

villains from whom no man was safe? And that although every man knows them to be the same as they were, and is equally afraid of, and would as little trust them as before they obtained a remission of their crimes?

My Lord Advocate has talked of their obtaining a new credit by the pardon. What is this, my Lords? Can it be a new credit to cheat and rob and plunder? Is this pardon to operate like a settlement in a banker's books, when he opens a new credit upon the next page, after old scores are cleared off?

My Lords, supposing that His Majesty really had this incomprehensible prerogative of changing by a sheet of parchment a corrupt and dishonest heart and cleansing it from all its impurities, I still maintain that it has not been exercised. Where is the clause in this pardon restoring Brown to his character and integrity? You have heard the pardon read, and there is no clause in it to that effect. He is screened against punishment and every effect of a prosecution. But it would have required a very express clause indeed to give the pardon the additional force of removing the infamy of his sentence, and surely the warmest advocates for prerogative cannot be offended at its being said that the King must exercise that prerogative before its power can be felt.

My Lords, I shall trouble you with nothing further upon this subject, which appears to me very clear. The sentence of the English Court is no more foreign than those to which the Courts of Scotland give effect every day. It is such a sentence as your Lordships would have pronounced had the crime been committed in this country. His Majesty's pardon cannot, by our law, restore this man from the infamy annexed to this sentence, and common reason tells us that it is beyond the power of kings, because it is beyond the power of man, to reinstate a man in his original integrity by their fiat.

He might as well have addressed the Salisbury Craigs. First to reply was Lord Hailes who considered himself something of an authority on the history of Scots law. He had pricked up his ears when Erskine cited what Sir George Mackenzie had once said. 'The Dean of Faculty has done more for Sir George Mackenzie than I was ever able to do,' he observed in his thin high-pitched voice, 'though I had studied him before the Dean of Faculty was born.' As if the affair in the bawdy-house down Halkerston's Wynd and the trial of the drunken Inspector of Hides had never been, Eskgrove and Swinton conceded that had Brown been convicted by a Scottish jury he could not now appear as a witness against the Deacon. Stonefield had nothing to say except that the objection should be thrown out.

Lastly, Braxfield spoke, and he trampled over Erskine's arguments. The Dean of Faculty had argued cleverly, he said, but if Ainslie was admissible, so was Brown; and that was an end of it. As Brown took the oath, his Irish voice answering Braxfield's broad Lanarkshire, Erskine and his friends would know that with this Bench the Deacon was done for.

Distantly the sound of the Tron Kirk's great brass bell came into the stifling courtroom; and gentlemen adjusted their watches to eight o'clock as the Dean of Faculty faced the Deacon's chief criminal accomplice.

But Erskine had met his match. Try as he might, he could not shake him. In his carefully rehearsed evidence, Brown confirmed all Ainslie had said about the break-in to the General Excise Office for Scotland, about the Deacon's part in the planning and the loaded pistols they used. And when Harry Erskine tried to sting him into confusion, the choleric Irishman lost his temper but gave nothing away.

'You're a clever chiel, John Broon,' mused Braxfield when the Dean of Faculty finally gave up. Clearer than any the old judge saw just how Brown had used the Deacon. On the run from the living oblivion of Botany Bay on the far side of the world, knowing that in crowded Edinburgh the Brodie gang must come to grief sooner or later, his had been the calculation that he could buy his freedom by betraying the Deacon. What precisely had been the bargain struck between Brown and the Sheriff's man, the Lord Justice Clerk neither knew nor perhaps wished to know. It might even be that Brown had egged on the Deacon to the big job at the General Excise Office, reckoning that in his desperation the Sheriff would barter his freedom for the gang leader's betrayal. The man's audacity was serving the cause of justice, ending the biggest threat to law and order that Edinburgh had known since the days of the Jacobites: for old Braxie that was enough.

For the Deacon, as he sat between the stalwarts of the City Guard, now to have his eyes opened to the use Brown had made of him must have been more than he could bear. The essential of Brodie-ism was at all times to have the whiphand over others. The lightning changes from City Father to arch-criminal, from the buck of the Cape to the family man of

Cant's Close all had this in common: the world must dance to the Deacon's fiddling. It was no part of the master plan that he should be the crutch by which an Irish crook on the run could hobble to safety.

For their part, the jury, crammed together, parched and dinnerless, if they still had their wits about them would be getting a novel insight of the man they thought they had known. Here was Brodie the romantic. John Brown told the Court that on the night of the Chessel's Court break-in, while the Deacon was handing out his pistols, he had burst into song: something about turning lead into gold. Keen theatre-goer that he was, Harry Erskine would recognize in this the high-wayman's song from the *The Beggar's Opera*.

> Hark I hear the sound of coaches,
> The hour of dark approaches,
> To your arms, brave boys and load . . .

And after Brown had stepped down from the witness box the jurors' eyes were opened by the letters the Deacon had entrusted to the Mid Calder tobacconist and which he had handed over to the Sheriff of Edinburgh; by these and by the unsigned letters found in the black travelling trunk that had accompanied him in his flight to the Low Countries. There would be some red faces on the public benches as Josie Norris read them out to the Court and so named the various friends who had helped the Deacon flee the country, the Rev. Mr Nairn,* the Grant relatives, and his bachelor cousin, Brodie of Milntown. It was this Morayshire laird who had rigged out the Deacon for his journey, insisting to his annoyance that old clothes were best. But the Laird of Milntown would not part with any money. 'I could not extract one guinea from him,' complained the Deacon, 'although he owes me twenty-four pounds for three years past.' The key figure in all this had been Walker, the attorney in the new Adelphi buildings off the Strand. He had given the Deacon enough money to see him through, and a letter of credit for all of fifty pounds to a firm of merchants in Philadelphia. The enforced emigrant was to turn up in the New World with funds to set himself up in business.

* Minister at the fishing burgh of Pittenweem in Fife, according to the *Fasti Ecclesiae Scotticanae*.

As the letters were read out in Court the Deacon would know only too well what was to come. If only he had taken his skin-flint cousin's advice, and not written to anyone until he was safely esconced in New York. But he hadn't. What was done was done.

And now old Josie Norris was coming to the fatal words. '*Whatever Brown and Ainslie may say, I had no hand in their depredations excepting the last.*' There it was. The jury had tumbled to the fatal admission. The goose was cooked.

Now the second letter he had penned on drink and loneliness in that Amsterdam beer-house was being read out. He had meant it for one of his cronies of the Cape, signing it with their cabalistic ritual. Now the whole world would know how deeply he felt for young Cicell in Cant's Close, what a torment was Jeannie Watt's waywardness ('She's a devil and a whore'). Last and worst, everyone would know what at heart he felt about himself. In his wretchedness that day in Amsterdam – seeking but not quite finding the word he wanted – he had penned his own epitaph at the foot of the letter. 'I often went in a retregard,' he had written, 'I have been all my life in a retregard motion.'

With daylight going, candles were lit and the Court settled to hear the prisoner's defence. In the city, lairds, merchants and lawyers set themselves to the evening's fun. 'Now some to porter, some to punch / some to their wife and some their wench . . .', while the rattling of the town drummer gave warning of the imminent deluge of slops from the high flats. By now, Lord Provost Grieve and the Town Council would be in their cups at Cleriheugh's. At the Isle of Man, the Cape would be in session too; and in both taverns there would be a fidget of impatience about the outcome of the trial. In George's Square as he prepared for his bed Mr Walter Scott, W.S., would be thinking of the drama in Parliament House; Braxfield was his neighbour and friend.

As Alexander Wight had intimated twelve hours past at the trial's beginning Brodie's defence was one of alibi. The Deacon's contention was that he had dined at home and then taken himself down Libberton's Wynd to sup, and sleep, with his second mistress.

Matthew Sheriff, the upholsterer of St James's Square, spoke stoutly for the first leg of the alibi, after Braxfield from the Bench had observed sourly that a brother-in-law to the 'pay-nell' must be a doubtful witness.

They dined at three, said Matthew Sheriff, drank together from then till ten, and he left the big house down Brodie's Close for Bunker's Hill* at eight.

THE LORD-ADVOCATE – Did you on your way home hear any clock strike or bell ring? How did you know that it was precisely a few minutes from eight o'clock when you left Mr Brodie?

MR SHERIFF – Ah dinna remember to hae heard ony clock strike or bell ring on ma' way home, but ah had a clock in ma' hoose an' a watch in ma' pocket. Ah marked the hoor frae Mr Brodie being sae immediately afterwards accused o' havin' that nicht broken intae the Excise Office, a thing which I did not then, and which I do not yet believe.

Ilay Campbell left it at that and Mistress Watt was called.

A story had got about that, in the Tolbooth, Brodie had gone through a form of marriage with Jean Watt. The Lord-Advocate was anxious to establish this. Perhaps the Defence had foreseen this move, and had forewarned her, for the lady of Libberton's Wynd was quick to deny that there had been a marriage.

On the night of the Excise Office break-in, the Deacon had come down the Wynd, she said, just as the eight o'clock bell was ringing. They were bedded by ten and slept together all night. Then a Miss Peggy Giles, who had been her servant and was now with the publican at Muttonhole,† confirmed the story. Her mistress and Brodie supped together about half an hour after eight o'clock on bread and beer and a piece of cheese which she was sent out to buy. The eight o'clock bell had been ringing from the Tron Kirk when Brodie came in. 'Mr Brodie often slept at ma' Mistress's hoose,' she added slyly.

Mistress Wallace, a neighbour down the steep defile of the

* Bunker's Hill was the name by which St James's Square was then known. News of the first battle of the American War had reached Edinburgh on the day on which the building of this the first square of the New Town was begun.
† Today a residential suburb, but known as Davidson's Mains.

Wynd, was called, It was a big occasion for her. Aeneas Morison put her words into very proper English, but putting it all back word for word into the patois of the Edinburgh housewife, what she said was:

Ah bide doon Libberton's Wynd and an ah ken Mr Brodie fine. Ah heard tell o' him leavin' Enbru' in March, and ah mind him comin' doon Jean Watt's stair jist at nine o'clock on the mornin' o' the Thursday afore he gaed away. Ah wis staunin' at my ain door at the fit o' the stair, an' ah had Francis Brodie by the haun', that's the Deacon's laddie.

As his faither passed him he pit a bawbee intae the bairn's haun an' clapped him on the heid. Aifter the Deacon was gane, ah said tae the bairn 'My pair wee laddie, you've missed seein' your daddie.' 'Nae, ah havenay,' he said, 'ma daddie was in the hoose a' nicht.'

Aifter ma man got his breakfast, ah went upstairs to Mistress Watt, an' ah said to her – jokin' like ye ken – 'you'll be a' richt the day, wi' the guidman in yer hoose a' nicht'. An' she says, says she, 'Aye, but pair man, he's no been well. He's an auffy sair throat.'

'How do you remember that this happened on the Thursday?' asked the Lord-Advocate.

'Ah can gie a reason a' richt, but ah dinna like tae mention it tae yer Lordships,' said Mrs Wallace.

'Tell us the reason, good woman,' said Eskgrove.

His prodigious judicial jaw, moving like a Dutch toy, cannot have frightened Mrs Wallace too much for she launched into her explanation forthwith.

Ye see, ah had bocht three pair o' shin on the Wednesday in the mairket. Ah mean a pair for each of ma' sons and one for ma' man. On Thursday mornin' ah missed ma' man's shin. Ah thocht they were stolen and ah was waitin' at the door at the time he usually got back for his breakfast – that wis aboot nine o'clock – to see if he kent ony thing o' them. If it had no been for this, ah wouldnay hae been at the door, nor would ah hae seen Mr Brodie come doon the stairs.

There were two more witnesses for Brodie. First, Charles Hay sought confirmation from Jamie Laing, the Depute Town Clerk, that Hamilton the master sweep had brought a process against the Deacon for using loaded dice in the evil little tavern off the Fleshmarket Close. The Defence game was to make plausible the contention that Brodie had fled for fear of prosecution at the instance of the master sweep.

Laing had the name of being a hard man and a hard drinker. He it was who put the Town Guard to work on summer nights digging up moudieworts in the Meadows. At his own hand, after the style of Ebenezer Balfour, he had once had some tipsy boys put aboard a ship in Leith Roads. By the time their heads cleared she was standing out beyond Inchkeith for the Americas.

This was his style, and he did not much relish getting involved in the Deacon's trial in any way.

MR HAY – Do you remember of any process being brought before the magistrates against Mr Brodie some time before he left the place for using false or loaded dice?

MR LAING – Ah do.

MR HAY – At whose instance was the process?

MR LAING – At the instance o' one Hamilton a chimney sweep in Portsburgh.*

MR HAY – When was this process?

MR LAING – Ah dinna exactly remember, but steps hae been taken in it within these six months.

LORD ESKGROVE – I suppose this Mr Hamil-tonn is not a comm-on sweep but a master who keeps men and boys for the pur-pose.

MR LAING – He is a maister, as your Lordship observes.

LORD-ADVOCATE – Do you know Mr Brodie to be a gambler?

MR LAING (anxious to be out of it) – Ah never gambled wi' *him*.

Then Robert Smith, the Deacon's foreman, established that picklocks were a cabinet-maker's tools of the trade, spring-saws the proper instruments for taking off a gamecock's spurs, and so there was no mystery in both being found in the search of Brodie's yard. Ilay Campbell conceded that this was so; no doubt he felt that he had more than enough for his address to the Jury.

Now there was an interval while the Defence Counsel withdrew to consult, Aeneas Morison having the privilege of listening in. And on the public benches there would be a great sucking of oranges and bringing out of whangs of cheese and chunks of

* The then down-at-heel suburb adjoining the west side of the city.

bread. Counsel (as will shortly be seen) also took the opportunity to refresh themselves.

It was a little past one in the morning when Ilay Campbell rose to speak, confident no doubt that supper and his warm bed in James's Court were not now too far off. This time Ilay Campbell spoke well. Of Smith he simply said that no witness had been produced in his favour, no alibi attempted. He had first made full admission of his part in the crimes of the Brodie gang, then at the last moment he had reneged. No more need to be said on that. But as to Brodie:

He is known to us all; educated as a gentleman; bred to a respectable business; and removed from suspicion from the rank he held amongst his fellow citizens. He was far above the reach of want and consequently of temptation; he had a lawful employment which might have enabled him to hold his station in society with respectability and credit; he has been more than once officially at the head of his profession, and was a member of the City Council. If therefore he, too, is guilty, his situation, in place of alleviating his guilt, is a high aggravation of it.

Then he set to work, moving from Brodie's admitted association with criminals and his craze for gambling to the circumstances of his flight from Edinburgh. There were the damning phrases in the letters found in the trunk which had travelled with him to Holland: the pistols and the dark lanthorn found in Brodie's yard; the flimsiness of the alibi – Jean Watt had either lied or mistaken the ten o'clock bell of the Magdalene Chapel in the Cowgate for the Tron Kirk bell at eight. Even without the evidence of his fellow criminals here was enough to warrant a conviction. With their clear account of Brodie's part in the planning and execution of the Excise Office break-in, the matter was beyond doubt. So he drew to a finish.

If the prisoner William Brodie, a person who from the nature of his employment had frequent opportunities of being introduced into the houses of others, has been guilty of the crime laid to his charge, and is allowed to escape punishment, the consequences to the inhabitants of this populous city may be of the most serious nature.

For this jury, a telling conclusion.

Small and lame, one leg so withered that it hung useless, his spectacles pushed above his bushy eyebrows, a shaggy terrier of a man, John Clerk rose to speak for George Smith. Sitting dejected in the dock, that big Englishman made a pathetic sight; professional con-man though he was, there was a measure of sympathy for him in the public galleries. He was no murderer like Brown the Irishman. He did have a dainty and apparently loving wife. He had been the first of the gang to make a full confession. There seemed to the general public no good reason why the Crown had selected him rather than one of his two criminal accomplices to take post beside Brodie in the dock.

It was now beyond his or anyone's skill to save Smith from the gallows, and Clerk knew it. But other purposes could be served.

By his lights, Braxfield had been fair. He had been at pains to point out that the jury must make up their own minds whether to believe Brown and Ainslie. But he had ruled, and in law rightly ruled, that there was no bar to their giving evidence. Yet the commonsense of the public galleries was with the Dean of Faculty when he argued that the Royal Pardon was now being used to violate the ancient laws of Scotland; that here was the pass to which the management of Scotland by the Dundas clique had led; and that this in the days to come when the demand for reform would become insistent and the threat to Dundas rule grow, was a dangerous weapon in their hands.

Braxfield had also shown a regrettable tendency to hustle young Mr Clerk. It may have been simply the discomfort of prolonged sitting on the Bench – Lord Auchinleck, James Boswell's father, once came near to killing himself by ignoring the imperatives of nature on a long trial like this. Whenever Clerk had cross-examined the Crown witnesses, Braxfield, glowering from the Bench, had sought to cut him short.

John Clerk was not so young as to be overawed by this. He had once hoped for a post in the India Office, but to all preferment Dundas was the key and the Clerk family at their elegant mansion house of Penycuik outside Edinburgh, jealous of their Midlothian rivals, did not choose to use it. Then he had shone in the famous Speculative Society at the University of Edinburgh, had become a Writer to the Signet, had mastered the modern science of accountancy, and at the age of twenty-eight had turned advocate. The Clerks of Penycuik were artistic and intellectual. John Clerk's father, the Liddell Hart of his day, thinking it futile that ships of the line should bang away at each other without decisive result, was writing a book on naval tactics which Rodney was to annotate and Nelson study (Trafalgar won in the Library of Penycuik House?). Just as given to hunting after ideas as the rest of the family was John Clerk's indolent and charming younger brother, at that time making a friend, a little below him in station, of the big fresh-faced son of Mr Walter Scott, W.S., of George's Square.

The fireworks display now about to enliven the Parliament House at two o'clock in the morning may have been touched off by the animosity the Clerks felt for the Dundases, the simple dislike of one county family for another. It may have been Whiggish outrage at Dundasism and its agent on the Bench, the gardener's grandson. Again, as Aeneas Morison was to remember, it may simply have been that at midnight John Clerk had downed a whole bottle of port and was now intent on showing off.* Perhaps all these combined in the baiting of Braxfield that now began.

'Gentlemen o' the jury,' said Clerk, beginning slowly as he always did, 'it's noo ma duty tae state the evidence tae you for the paynell, Mister Smith, an' I shall trouble ye wi a verra few observations only.'

First he tamped the explosive. 'John Broon, ye're a clever chiel,'† Braxfield had said to the Irishman in wary admiration that this the blackest of villains had had the wit to see how the Crown might wish to use him. It was unwise of my Lord Justice Clerk so to have spoken. To cheers from the public benches Clerk now contrasted the Cowgate grocer and his loving wife with Brown the Irish scoundrel, 'wha' you'll mind was sae highly complimented by their Lordships when he left the box'.

Braxfield was quick to take his meaning. 'Be short and concise, sir, at this time o' the mornin',' he barked. 'Pray your Lordship, let me proceed,' said Clerk.

So the young advocate insolently took his time, reviewing the evidence, explaining away Smith's confession of guilt with preposterous rhetoric.

A fit o' temporary frenzy, an insanity, grippet him, and he accused himsel' o' an atrocious crime as the only means o' safety. But this accusation is rejected by his cooler judgment . . .

---

* Nearer a half-bottle in quantity by present-day measurement, but fortification enough.
† Chiel: fellow.

And so on. Then he lit the short fuse.

I come next tae the testimony o' Ainslie an' Brown. Gentlemen, you hae heard a variety o' objections stated to the admissabeelity o' their evidence – all of which has been overruled by the Court. But notwithstanding the judgment o' their Lordships, I must adhere tae these objeetions and maintain that they ocht no to hae been admitted as wutnesses. Gentlemen ah' think a great deal o' maist improper evidence has been received in this case for the Croon.

The Bench exploded.

THE LORD JUSTICE CLERK – Dae ye say that, sir, aifter the judgment which the court has pronounced? That, sir, is a maist improper observation tae the jury.

LORD STONEFIELD – It's a positive reflection on the Court.

LORD HAILES – It's a flat accusation that we have admitted improper evidence.

LORD ESKGROVE – I ne-ver heard the like of this from any young coun-sel at the be-ginn-ing of his car-eer at this bar.

THE LORD JUSTICE CLERK – Wi thae admoneetions, gang on, sir; proceed, sir.

MR CLERK – Aweel, my Lords, if I go on, I beg to assail at the outset the evidence of thae twa corbies* or infernal scoondrels, Ainslie and Brown.

THE LORD JUSTICE CLERK – Tak' care, sir, what you say.

MR CLERK – Yes, my Lords, I say that they are baith maist infamous characters. Gentlemen, ye should discard sic vagabonds, an' no' rely on their evidence in ony way. Gin ye knock oot the vile brains o' their evidence in this case, there is naethin' else remainin' on which ye can convict ma pair client, except his ain verra candid declarations which I hae already explained to you. Gentlemen, these nefarious wutnesses Ainslie and Brown, should hae stood at this bar this nicht in place o' my client, wha was happy in his domestic preevacy wi' his pair, honest, inoffending wife, whom ye this day saw – an' ma hairt bleeds for her.

The public benches erupted in applause; it was quickly suppressed.

Wi respect tae this said Mister John Brown alias Humphry Moore, you had it oot o' his ain mooth that he was a convicted felon in England, an' I say to you that nae convicted felon ocht, by the good and glorious law o' Scotland, tae be received as a wutness in this or any other case in the British domeenions.

* Corbie: a hoodie-crow (which picks out the eyes of young lambs).

D

More cheers and clapping; and shouts of 'Silence' from the Macers.

THE LORD JUSTICE CLERK – Mr Clerk, please restrict yer reflections. The Court hae admitted the wutness.

ME CLERK – Yes, my Lords, I ken that verra weel, but your Lordships should no' hae admitted him, and o' that the jury will now judge.

THE LORD JUSTICE CLERK – This is maist indecent behaviour. You canna be allowed to speak to the admissibeelity; to the credibeelity ye may.

LORD STONEFIELD – This young man is again attacking the Court.

MR CLERK – No, my Lords, Ah'm no attackin' the Court. Ah'm attackin' that villain o' a wutness, wha I tell your Lordships, is no' worth his value in hemp.

THE LORD JUSTICE CLERK – The Court, sir, hae already solemnly decided, as you ken, that in law the objections tae thae wutnesses should be repelled, and so they were repelled; therefore you should hae naethin' mair to say to us on that point.

Henry Erskine got to his feet. Had he known what Clerk would be up to? It would be hard to believe that he was entirely in the dark. Now he suggested that his younger colleague might desist since he, as Dean of Faculty, intended to speak to the point later. Perhaps, as Erskine had foreseen, Clerk turned a deaf ear to this.

MR CLERK – But, my Lords, the jury *are* tae judge o' the law as weel as the facts.

THE LORD JUSTICE CLERK – Sir, I tell you that the jury hae naethin' tae dae wi' the law, but to tak' it *simpliciter* frae me.

MR CLERK – That I deny.

Hubbub in court.

LORD HAILES – Sir, will you deny the authority of this High Court?

MR CLERK – Gentlemen of the jury, notwithstanding o' this interruption, I beg to tell you, wi a' confidence and a' respect, that you are the judges o' the law as weel as o' the facts. You are the judges o' the hale.

THE LORD JUSTICE CLERK – Ye're talkin' nonsense, sir.

MR CLERK – Ma Lord, you had better no' snub me in this way. I never mean tae speak nonsense.

THE LORD JUSTICE CLERK (flabbergasted) – Proceed – gang on, sir.

Clerk would know very well that it was for the judges, not the jury, to decide whether a witness be admitted. He was speaking for political effect. To storm like this at the Bastille of the Dundas establishment was the popular cause. And if he kept on a little longer the Law Officers might even play into his hands. They might unwisely try to justify this increase in the royal power and prerogative.

MR CLERK – Gentlemen, I was telling you that this infernal wutness wis convicted o' felony in England. How dare he come here tae be received as a wutness in this case!

And Ilay Campbell walked into the trap.

THE LORD-ADVOCATE – He has, as I have shown you, received His Majesty's free pardon.
MR CLERK – Yes, so I see. But, gentlemen o' the jury, I ask you, on your oaths, *can* His Majesty's mak' a tainted scoondrel an honest man?

Great applause in Court: this was what the Edinburgh Whigs had come to hear.

THE LORD JUSTICE CLERK – Macers, clear the Court if there's ony mair unruly din.
THE LORD-ADVOCATE (going further into the trap and addressing Clerk) – Sir, permit me to say, after this interruption, that the prerogative of mercy is the brightest jewel in His Majesty's Crown.
MR CLERK (deliberately, and looking straight at the Campbell Lord-Advocate and the Dundas Solicitor General) – I hope his Majesty's Crown will never been contaminated by *ony* villains aroon' it.

Sensation in Court: the judges beside themselves with indignation.

THE LORD JUSTICE CLERK (to Ilay Campbell) – Dae ye want his words noted doon?
THE LORD-ADVOCATE – Oh no, my Lord, not exactly yet. My young friend will soon cool in his effervescence for his client.
THE LORD JUSTICE CLERK – (to Clerk, and still at a loss what to do) – Gang on, young man.
MR CLERK – Gentlemen of the jury, I was jist saying to you, when this outbreak on the bench occurred, that you were the judges o' the law and o' the facts in this case.
THE LORD JUSTICE CLERK – We canna tolerate this, sir. It is an

indignity tae this High Court – a verra gross indignity, deservin'
of the severest reprobation.

MR CLERK – My Lords, I know that your Lordships hae determined
this question, but the jury hae not. They are judges baith o' fact
and o' the law, and are no' bound by your Lordships' determination, unless it agrees with their ain opeenion. Unless ah'm allowed
tae speak tae the jury in this manner, ah'm determined no tae
speak a word mair. Ah'm willin tae sit doon gin your Lordships
command me.

Clerk seated himself, and folded his arms. 'Gang on, sir, gang
on to the length of your tether,' sneered Braxfield. Clerk did
just that.

MR CLERK – Yes, gentlemen, I staun up here as an *independent*
Scottish advocate, and I tell ye, a jury o' ma countrymen, that
you are the judges o' the law as weel as o' the facts.

THE LORD JUSTICE CLERK – Beware of whit ye are aboot, sir.

Clerk sat down and refused to continue.

THE LORD JUSTICE CLERK – Are you done, sir, wi' your speech?

MR CLERK – No, ma Lord, ah'm no done.

THE LORD JUSTICE CLERK – Then gang on, sir, at your peril.

LORD HAILES (weary, and wanting only an end to the pantomime) –
You had better go on, Mr Clerk. Do go on.

MR CLERK – This has been too often repeated. I hae met with nae
politeness frae the Court. You hae interrupted me, you hae
snubbed me rather too often ma' Lord, in the line o' ma defence.
Ah maintain that the jury are judges o' the law as weel as o' the
facts; an ah'm positively resolved that ah'll gang nae further
unless ah'm allowed tae speak in ma ain way.

THE LORD JUSTICE CLERK – Then we must noo ca' upon the Dean
o' Faculty tae proceed wi' his address for the prisoner Brodie,
which the Court will hear wi' the greatest attention.

But Erskine shook his head.

'Verra weel. The Court will proceed noo an' discharge its
duty'. And Braxfield made to begin his charge to the jury,
bidding them rise to their feet.

MR CLERK (starting to his feet and shaking his fist at the Bench) –
Hang ma' client gin ye daur, my Lord, without hearin' me in his
defence!

Pandemonium in the galleries; consternation on the Bench;
Aeneas Morison unable to believe his ears – or his eyes, because

Braxfield and his colleagues were now retreating from the Bench to consult what to do. Surely it must be to clap John Clerk into the Tolbooth.

But when they filed back into Court it was seen that Clerk had won. Suppressing his rage, Braxfield asked him to finish his address to the jury in his own way. The Lord Justice Clerk lived by the rule of law: it bound him too.

Clerk had not much more to say. He played a little on minor inconsistencies in the Crown evidence but said he would leave it to the Dean of Faculty to show why Brown and Ainslie should not be believed at all. He had made his point about their ever having been admitted and was content to leave it at that. And so he sat down.

There had never been anything like it in the High Court of Justiciary. There was never to be anything like it again. But the young advocate had acted with the same irresponsibility with which he fathered and ignored bastards.* It may have crossed the Deacon's mind that with this Bench the sentence was a foregone conclusion; that the choice was now between the Tolbooth gallows and Botany Bay; and that the chooser would be Henry Dundas. Young Mr Clerk's fireworks display would not make Great Hal any more likely to come to the aid of Deacon Brodie.

Three o'clock in the dark city; the crown of St Giles looking through the gloom to the steeple of the Tron; in the lighted courtroom Henry Erskine rose to address the jury.

'Dinna be brief, Harry, dinna be brief,' old Lord Polkemmet had once interrupted from the Bench when Erskine had said he would make only a brief speech. To connoisseurs of rhetoric brought up on Scotch sermons, an Erskine speech was a treat. Even the ladies would make up parties to hear him plead. That night no one would leave until he had had his fling. *Forbye* as they would say, for entrance fee they had each had to press all of five shillings into the doorkeeper's horny hand.

Erskine now gave them their money's worth. He quoted from the tragedy of *Douglas,* so popular at the Theatre Royal:

* For an amusing anecdote of how two such – sons to two sisters in the mining village of Midlothian – made themselves known to Clerk in later years, see *The Carles of Edinburgh,* by John Heiton, 1852.

> The needy man who has known better days,
> One whom distress has spited at the world,
> Is he whom tempting friends would pitch upon,
> To do such deeds, as make the prosperous men,
> Lift up their hands and wonder who could do them.

and conceded that the Deacon did not fall into this category.
Brodie was a gambler, said the Dean of Faculty, and he quoted
Shakespeare.

> The very head and front of his offending,
> Has this extent; no more.

Accept this said Harry Erskine and all his actions were explic-
able.

He protested that he had not been allowed to prove that a
bargain had been struck between Ainslie and Sheriff Cockburn.
And against Brown he turned all his skill in words and imagery.

The evidence of Brown is, if possible, still more unworthy of credit
than that of Ainslie. A more hardened and determined villain can
hardly be figured. You saw, gentlemen, the manner in which he
gave his evidence. He appeared more like a man rehearsing and
expatiating upon the patriotic acts he had performed for the good
of his country than a criminal unfolding the black history of his
own iniquities.

He has no doubt received His Majesty's pardon. It has been
obtained for him, at a very great expense, for the sole purpose of
enabling him to be a witness in this cause. But though the Court
has determined that this pardon, the crimes being committed in
England, rehabilitates this man, and that his evidence is admissible;
yet no pardon can restore his credibility, or render him an honest
man. The pardon cannot alter the nature of the criminal. Can the
Ethiopian change his skin, or the leopard his spots? Is it possible
that the King's pardon can restore purity of heart, rectitude, and
integrity? Can a piece of parchment with a seal dangling at its
foot turn wickedness into honesty, and transmute infamy into
honour? The King has no such prerogative. This is the prerogative
of the King of Kings alone, exerted only towards repenting offen-
ders; and even with him such change may well be accounted a
miracle.

In the eye of reason, therefore, Brown is still a notorious convicted
felon, an infamous, unrepenting villain, who, till the 28th July last,
the date of the pardon, would not have been received as a witness
even in a twopenny-halfpenny cause between man and man.
And yet upon this evidence is now to depend the reputation and

life of a once respected citizen! These things need only to be mentioned, gentlemen, in order to be fully felt, nor will I insult the understanding of so intelligent a jury by dwelling upon them for a moment longer.

But this, gentlemen, is not all. Mark the game which this man had to play, and in what manner he has played it. He had not, like Ainslie, only his accession to this offence to shake himself loose of. A sentence of transportation hung over his head. This sentence he has not obeyed; and the penal certification is in England, I suppose, as it is with us, capital. By accusing a person of such consequence as to make it worth the while of the servants of the Crown to make him King's evidence, he not only frees himself from trial for the offences committed here, but secured a pardon for the offence of which he stood convicted, as it was necessary to qualify him to be a witness that his former conviction be done away, and all his former crimes washed off in the fountain of Royal favour. A bribe of such magnitude flesh and blood could not resist. Thus, gentlemen, in addition to the profligacy of character, to the load of infamy under which this man laboured, you see the most powerful engines which can set in motion the human soul employed to drag him forward to an accusation which he had not originally made, for which, but for this, his conscience, hardened as it is, might have prevented him from ever making.

As Erskine presented it, the Deacon's alibi was almost believable. He made much of the integrity of Mr Sheriff of St James's Square, 'a gentleman well known to many of you as a man of character and reputation, in a rank of life equal to many of yourselves'. If Matthew Sheriff must be believed, then the criminal's description of the goings on in Smith's house as the gang assembled for the raid was so much moonshine. If they could lie about this particular, their whole evidence could be a pack of falsehoods.

He made a brave show of dismissing the Deacon's implied confession of guilt to 'the last fatal depredation' in the unsigned letter from the travelling chest. This, he said, was nothing more than a reference to the tussle over loaded dice with the master chimney sweep in Clark's Tavern. Nor was there anything sinister in the dark lantern found in the cockpens down Brodie's Close. 'It is well known,' said Erskine, 'that cocks are fed by candlelight.'

So the superb performance was brought to an end, as the candles flickered away in the crowded courtroom.

In the hands of an upright and intelligent jury [he concluded], I
leave this unfortunate gentleman confident that whatever verdict
you shall pronounce will be the result of your ripest judgment,
tempered, in case of doubt, with that tenderness with which it
becomes you to decide when the fame and life of a fellow-citizen
are at stake.

It had all been delivered without a single note; and any flame
of hope it kindled in the Deacon, the Lord Justice Clerk was
quick to extinguish.

His face screwed up with the intensity of his reasoning,
Braxfield gave the jury their instructions in the plainest terms.
No bargain had been proved between Ainslie and the Crown.
He and Brown were good witnesses, their evidence corro-
borating each other, and this in turn was buttressed by Smith's
(recanted) admission of guilt.

Brodie's flight and the scrolls found in his travelling trunk
admitted only one interpretation. Jean Watt was not to be
believed. 'Ye are to conseeder, gentlemen, that although, to
be shair, she's no his wife, yet she is his mistress. And luve is
aften as deeply rooted between folk o' that kidney as between
lawfu' man an' wife.

'Takin' a' the circumstances the gether,' he went on, 'I hae
nae doubt in ma ain mind that Mister Brodie was there at the
breakin' in tae the Excise Office. As to the ither man Smith,
there can be nae doubt at a' aboot him. If you're o' the same
opeenion, gentlemen, you'll return a verdict against baith the
prisoners. But gin you're o' a different opeenion, an' dinna
consider the evidence against Brodie strang eneuch, you'll
bring in a verdict accordingly.'

It was now six o'clock, the Crown of St Giles purple with the
rising sun, the waters piped from distant Comiston washing the
steep streets; in the tall lands, a thousand servant lassies stirring
a thousand porridge pots.

'An', gentlemen,' Braxfield concluded, peering over his
spectacles, 'I want ye back here wi' your verdict by twelve
o'clock.'

The Court met again after noon, the weary jurors having
begged Braxfield for an extra hour that they might at least
have the refreshment of the midday dram. Now in the middle

of that August day back from the Tolbooth came George Smith and the Deacon to be brought to the Bar. There followed the usual, awful solemnities. The verdict was handed over in an envelope sealed with black wax. First Braxfield opened it and read the finding, then Eskgrove, then Hailes, Stonefield and Swinton. The crowded courtroom was dead silent. Old Josie Norris then read aloud the unanimous finding of guilty against the two. 'It is now incumbent on me, my Lords, to move your Lordships to pronounce the sentence of law against the prisoners at the Bar,' said Ilay Campbell. Now that the verdict was given it would only be humane to get the business of the day over and done with quickly.

But there was one last shot in the Defence locker. Early on in the trial John Clerk had established a fact which might just save the day. 'Pray, Mr Thomson,' he had said to the Accountant of Excise in the cross-examination, 'was the Excise Office, when in the Canongate, kept in one house or in two houses?' It was kept in one large house, but also in a smaller building nearly adjoining it, was the reply. Ainslie on the night of the break-in had, in fact, skulked in the angle of the two buildings.

The indictment, Clerk had been quick to notice, spoke only of 'the house in which the General Excise Office of Scotland was then kept'. House singular. And it was a cardinal principle of the criminal law of Scotland that indictments must be tightly drawn. So to the Defence's last fling.

MR WIGHT – My Lords, before your Lordships proceed to pronounce judgment, I have an objection to state on behalf of the prisoners at the bar which, in my opinion, ought to prevent any judgment from passing upon this verdict. My Lords, from the evidence taken in the course of this trial, it appears that the libel is insufficient, in so far as it charges 'that the pannels did wickedly and feloniously break into the house in which the General Excise Office for Scotland, was then kept' whereas it ought to have stated that they so broke into one of the houses so kept, describing such house particularly. For it appears from the proof that there were two separate and distinct houses in which the General Excise Office for Scotland was then kept, on the opposite sides of the court, and at a considerable distance from each other.

THE LORD-ADVOCATE – My Lords, I am not a little surprised that an objection of this nature should be brought forward at this time. If the gentlemen on the other side of the bar meant to have stated any such objection as the present, they ought to have done it yesterday. But after they have allowed the indictment to pass without any such objection; after your Lordships have sustained it as relevant, and remitted it to the knowledge of an assize in common form; and when the jury have returned a verdict finding the prisoners guilty of the crime charged – there can be no room for any further proceeding, except to pronounce the sentence of the law upon the verdict so returned.

It would have been better that Ilay Campbell had left it at that. But he had foreseen the coming of this objection and armed himself with some useful facts. Nor could he neglect this chance to outshine Harry Erskine.

But my Lords, the objection itself is altogether frivolous, for the house that was broke into, as stated in the indictment, was really and truly the house known by the name of the General Excise Office for Scotland at the time. It is indeed true that one or two of the clerks and inferior officers were accommodated in a small house within a few feet or yards of the large one, and which was joined to it by a wall like a wing. But this did not make them in any sense of the word two separate houses. The principal house which was broke into, was hired at £300 per annum of rent, and the small house at £8 per annum. This last was just as much a part of the General Excise Office as a kitchen separate from any house is a part of that house. And surely your Lordships would not cast an indictment which charged that a man's house was broke into, upon the ground that his kitchen was not joined to his house, which very often happens. I therefore, my Lords, consider this as a very frivolous objection, and I know that the honourable counsel on the other side of the bar knows too well the dignity of his character and the honour of his profession to insist seriously upon an objection so futile. Had this been the case of a poor man, my Lord, we would not have heard of this objection, and I do not see what title the rank and situation of this man can plead for troubling the Court with frivolous objections to the verdict of a jury after so long and so fair a trial.

His golfing friends would say that the Lord-Advocate had been pressing on his swing.

DEAN OF FACULTY – My Lords, I know what belongs to the dignity of my profession and the honour of my character as well as my Lord-Advocate.

Hand on his heart Ilay Campbell interrupted to expostulate that he meant to say nothing disrespectful to the Dean of

Faculty. Braxfield cut short the play-acting. Erskine continued:

My Lords, I say that I know how I ought to conduct myself, both as a lawyer and a gentleman, and it is in the full conviction of performing my duty that I rise to enforce the present objection, which I think is such a one as ought to overturn this verdict.

It has been asked why this objection was not brought forward in an earlier stage of the trail – why it was not pleaded at the very outset, as sufficient to cast the indictment? It has been called a frivolous objection to my Lord Advocate. But many objections were styled frivolous by the gentlemen on that side of the table during the course of this trial, which your Lordships decided to be well founded. My Lords, it was impossible to plead it in this early stage, because the fact came out to be as stated in the objection only during the time that the proof in this trial was led.

With regard to the matter of fact in this case, I shall not detain your Lordships a moment. Nothing is clearer from the evidence than that there were two separate and distinct houses in which the Excise Office was kept at the time when the robbery was committed. Several of the witnesses have sworn to this, and it was admitted on the other side of the table. I therefore say, my Lords, that this verdict, which has found the prisoners guilty of breaking into the house in which the General Excise Office was kept, finds nothing.

It is in vain to say that these two houses belonged to one and the same office. If they are not under the same roof – which it is confessed these two houses are not – then it is of no importance how near they may be to each other, for neither of them is the house in which the Excise Office was kept, but only one of the houses employed for that purpose. His Grace the Duke of Buccleugh has two houses lying near each other, the house of Dalkeith and the house of Smeiton, both in the parish of Dalkeith. Would the verdict of a jury be good, which, upon the statement of an indictment that the house of the Duke of Buccleugh, lying within the parish of Dalkeith, was broke into, should simply find the pannel guilty? Surely not. It would be necessary to specify which of the houses was broke into, because an innocent man, who could prove an alibi with regard to the one, might not be able to prove it with regard to both, or, in short, because the libel is uncertain.

The Excise Office is now removed to the house lately possessed by Sir Laurence Dundas in the New Town of Edinburgh. Suppose that part of the offices still remained in the former place, would it be sufficient to say that the house in which the General Excise Office is kept was broke into, when there were evidently two houses in which it was kept, one in the Old and one in the New Town? And the only difference betwixt that case and the present is that the distance is greater, for in both cases the houses are equally separate and distinct.

In the same way, for the sake of illustration, it was not till lately that I myself could find a house sufficiently convenient both for the purposes of business and accommodation of a numerous family. I had accordingly two houses, one in George Square and one in Princes Street, and I have done business in both of them. Now, would an indictment charging a person with having broken into the house of the Honourable Henry Erskine, Dean of the Faculty of Advocates, be sufficient, while I possessed two houses, to support a verdict which found the pannel in general terms guilty? It would not be enough to say that I employed both houses frequently for the same purposes, and that I could pass from the one into the other, though not without some little inconvenience of getting wet when it rained. This undoubetdly would not be sufficient, unless I could prove that both houses were one and the same; a verdict finding the pannel guilty of breaking into the house, could, from its uncertainty, apply neither to the one nor to the other.

My Lords, I will not detain your Lordships. The case is very short and simple, and without stating any further illustrations or arguments, I think that the prisoner cannot be more safe than in the opinions which your Lordships shall deliver upon so plain a point so fairly stated to you.

It was a commendable attempt, the final lunge in his easy, allusive style. But it would not do. 'The Dean of Faculty is mistaken with regard to the houses possessed by the Duke of Buccleugh,' piped Hailes, His Grace's Midlothian neighbour. 'They are not both in the parish of Dalkeith, as the house of Smeiton lies in the parish of Inveresk.' Having put Erskine right about that, he pointed to the obvious. There was a world of difference between two separate houses and an Office with its overflow. Eskgrove agreed. Sensitive old soul that he was he looked at the Deacon whose face had brightened as Harry Erskine got under way and advised him not to make things harder for himself by hoping for this last-minute reprieve.

Stonefield said sniffily, 'I dinna understaun' them bringin' forward this objection. Do they want tae introduce the forms o' the law o' England?' With careful logic Swinton insisted that the verdict must stand. 'Why did our ancestors establish the rules of proceeding which we have always observed? It was for the security of the lives and liberties of the subjects of this

Kingdom. The security handed down to us from our ancestors, we are bound to deliver unimpaired to posterity.'

With his massive commonsense Braxfield had the last word.

'The Objection ocht tae hae been stated in the pleadin' as a bar tae the present trial,' he said, 'and the coonsel for the paynells ocht then tae hae brocht forward whatever proof they had. It's noo impossible for the Court tae review the evidence which has been led. The objection maun be repelled. My Lords, you'll noo gie yer opeenions aboot the sentence tae be pronounced agin' the paynells at the bar.'

They should be carried back to the Tolbooth, there detained and executed on Wednesday the first day of October, said Hailes.

'I sin-cerely comm-is-erate the fate of these un-happy men,' said Eskgrove. 'One of them es-pec-ially I pity much. Now that I see him at the Bar, I re-coll-ect having known him in his better days and I re-mem-ber his father who was one most worthy, and honourable, and respected man.'

Hang them, said Stonefield. Swinton sought more decorous words, but the sentiment was the same.

'William Brodie an' George Smith,' said Braxfield, 'it belongs tae ma' office tae pronoonce the sentence o' the law agin' ye. Ye hae had a lang an' fair trial, conducted on the pairt o' the public prosecutor wi' the utmost candour an' humanity. Ye've been assisted wi' able coonsel, whae hae exerted the greatest abeelity an' fidelity in yer defence.'

Clerk might be a whipper-snapper but Harry Erskine was Braxie's friend.

Then being a truly great man, he spoke with a directness of compassion to the Deacon, the son of old Francis.

Ah wish ah could be of ony use tae you in yer melancholy situation. You, William Brodie, frae yer education and habits o' life, canna but ken a' thing aboot yer present situation which ah could suggest tae you. It's much tae be lamented that thae vices, which are called gentlemanly vices, are sae favourably looked upon in the present age. They hae been the source o' yer ruin; and, whatever may be thocht o' them, they are sic as assuredly lead tae ruin. I hope you'll improve the short time which ye hae noo' tae live by reflectin' upon yer past conduct, and endeavourin' tae procure, by a sincere repentence, forgiveness for yer money crimes. Goad aye listens tae those wha' seek him wi' sincerity.

And so he pronounced the sentence of death. By custom there had to be an interval of time to allow the Home Secretary – and Henry Dundas – to consider any plea for a reprieve by exercise of the King's prerogative of mercy. (For sentences of death passed on the Northern Circuit, to allow for the greater distances to and from Whitehall, the span of time had to be longer.) But that, old Braxie would be sure, was only a formality. On the first day of October, Brodie and Smith would be taken from the Tolbooth to the place of execution; there 'betwixt the hoors of twa an' four o'clock aifter noon tae be hingit by the necks, by the hauns o' the Common Executioner upon the gibbet until they be deid'.

The trial was over. Attention now moved abruptly from the legal gladiators. All eyes were now on the Deacon. He stood erect, one hand by his side, the other at his lapel. Aeneas Morison saw him make as if to speak but that Erskine restrained him. So he simply bowed to the judges, yet he must have been in a frenzy of exasperation, for he kicked the blubbering Smith as the latter was hauled away. If only that fool had kept quiet, none of this need have happened. And why did Harry Erskine stop me making my exit in style?

3

The Deacon's
Transmogrification

The trial over, Harry Erskine was off to Almondell in his smart yellow coach. But first he had a letter from Willie Creech to answer. Could Mr Creech be favoured with a sight of the Dean of Faculty's notes? With just a hint of impatience he answered that there were none. His speeches had all been *ex tempore*.

That afternoon Creech crossed the High Street to the bachelor comfort of his house at the head of Craig's Close, sure in his mind that justice had been done. The Deacon was nothing more than a gambler who had taken to crime. One vice had led to another. 'Read this and tremble, ye who 'scape the laws', he was to quote from Alexander Pope on the title page of the '*Account of the Trial of William Brodie and George Smith by William Creech One of the Jury*' which, price three shillings, was to be on sale in the big shop in the Luckenbooths within the week. In the introduction, this prim publisher of blameless life – except in having been slow to pay the poet Burns – let fly:

Of all the vices of dissipated life, none perhaps is more fascinating, or more destructive to self repose, to virtue, and to industry than *gaming*.

To those, whose life has been destined to attention and industry, this vice is of all others the most pernicious. He who builds his hopes of wealth on his good fortune at play, will seldom plod in the road of honest industry and duty. Why should he toil in business to obtain shillings and pence, when he may gain pounds in pleasurable amusement? Such is his delusion, and it is thus his mind becomes unfitted for his station. Unsuccessful play plunges him into distress, impels him to dishonesty; and a mind harassed with inquietude seeks relief in means the most base and dishonourable.

It is thus that the mind, which, like the placid summer sea, might have reflected the bright serenity of Heaven is frequently found to resemble the ocean, tossed by the dark storms of December.

This moralizing will not altogether do. The Deacon had somehow dissipated most of the fortune of £10 000 which old Francis had left him. But his books had balanced; he knew to the last penny how he stood; and his business was prospering.

One of the papers found in the fatal travelling chest in his Amsterdam lodgings was 'A state of my affairs as near as I can make out at present from memory'. The jury, said Creech, had too much delicacy to inspect it. Had they done so they would have seen that bonds to Sister Jean and Sister Jamie, to the Reverend Mr John Nairn and to Sir William Forbes, the town's chief banker, came to £2750. Against this stood the tenement in Horse Wynd off the foot of the Canongate, 'the new fore tenement at the Netherbow', the tenement of five storeys in the World's End Close, and the two storeys in the Bank Close near Parliament House. These with bills due, and the value of his stock in trade – 'ready made furniture, glasses finished and unfinished, hair and hair cloth, brass and iron work, silvering utensils, benches and shope tools, mahogany and other woods, ready made doors and windows' – gave him a handsome balance of £1422 (which multiply by twelve at least to bring to present-day value). Avid for play the Deacon may have been, but until the 5th of March he had gone about his business as usual.

If gambling was not the whole reason, what then? How dedicated a criminal was he? The Edinburgh public were now in for a severe shock about the scale of his crimes. In the grim old Tolbooth, awaiting execution, the wretched Smith disclosed the Brodie gang's programme for 1788. Dalgleish and Dickie, watchmakers, White and Mitchell, lottery office keepers, 'a rich baker' near Brodie's Close, and a linen draper's in the Lawnmarket were all to be done. The Town Council Chamber was to be raided for the mace and the Chamberlain's Office for money. The Bank of Scotland was to be broken into; and the Stirling Stage Coach, carrying £1000 to pay the Carron workmen, to be plundered.

It seems unlikely that George Smith, the prospect of hanging concentrating his thoughts wonderfully, would make up this list out of his imagination. Rather it shows the fertility of the

Deacon's mind. Day and daily in the dirty low-roofed Council Chamber he had sat below the town's mace. It was at the Bank of Scotland off Parliament Close that he kept his money. Close friends in the Carron Company he must have had, for it was to them he turned when he had to flee the country: the *Endeavour* sloop was a Carron boat. And the rich baker in Brodie's Close was his next door neighbour. Throughout the pattern was the same; acquaintance and friendship as well as the duplicates cut in Brodie's yard were the keys that so mysteriously opened doors. All this was dangerous, potentially violent, crime. The Brodie gang went armed to Chessel's Court, and had they continued this would have been their style.

With time running out and the fatal 1st of October coming near, Willie Creech was still puzzled by the enigma of the Deacon. Perhaps he now saw for himself that it would not do to put it all down to a passion for gaming. Perhaps the first edition of his book having sold out in a few days he thought he might usefully extend the second. And so he began to put together a narrative of the Deacon's last days.

The situation of criminals in the prison of Edinburgh, after condemnation is peculiarly irksome [he wrote]. They are chained by one leg to a bar of iron,* alongside of which they may walk; and their bed is made by the side of it. Mr Brodie was allowed a longer chain than usual, a table and chair, with pen, ink, and paper; and the visits of any of his friends and acquaintances he wished to see, till the night before his execution, when none were permitted to visit him but clergymen.

Some of his closer friends who now visited him were as anxious as Creech to record the Deacon's behaviour. They too were aware that they were in the presence of an extraordinary man. Their reports were that the Deacon talked much of having wanted to join the Navy when he was a lad. Then he would have come to honour, not to this. (Mr Midshipman Brodie accepting the sword of a French *lieutenant de frégate*? Captain Brodie, R.N., being received by Rodney for his gallant part in the Battle of the Saints? In deciding a career for his elder son, old Francis, skilled cabinet-maker that he was, should have known better than fit a square peg into a round hole.)

* Known as 'the Gaud'.

He was, they reported, for the most part wonderfully com-
posed. He was given to making little jokes about his situation;
said that he was about to take a leap in the dark; that the
fellows putting up the scaffold made a noise like shipbuilders
but that his voyage would be a short one; and that the Excise
had made a ridiculous fuss about the loss of a very little money.
But he was exasperated by the tearful ways of his fellow dis-
ciples of 'the Gaud', and commented pungently about the
clergy ever in and out of the Iron Room in search of a soul to
save.

This combination of fortitude and exasperation Creech also
noted. His narrative continues:

To the same bar of iron on which he was chained, were, on this
singular occasion, George Smith, and two men condemned for
robbing the Dundee Bank.* Brodie was offered a separate room,
but declined it. Smith was uniformly fervent in religious exercises.
Brodie said, upon some of these occasions, that he was so much
employed with his temporal concerns, he could not attend to them;
but, when his business was finished, he would hear the clergymen.
At times, however, he conversed with the clergy, and joined in their
devotions. His conversation upon these occasions was directed to
the principles of natural religion, not to the doctrines of revelation.
On Friday before his execution, he was visited by his daughter, a
fine girl of about ten years of age. The feelings of the father gave
strong proofs of his sensibility; he embraced her with emotion, and
blessed her with affection.
On the Sunday preceding his execution, a respite of six weeks
arrived for Falconer and Bruce, the two people condemned for
robbing the Dundee Bank. The news made Brodie more serious for
a little time than he had before been; and he expressed his satis-
faction at the event. Smith said 'Six weeks is but a short period'. Brodie,
with emotion, answered, 'George, What would you and I give for six
weeks longer? Six weeks would be an age to us!'

On Sundays he would go with the other prisoners to the
Tolbooth Church, one of the kirks into which the old fabric of
St Giles was divided, there to sing psalms, the precentor, in the
old Scotch style, leading line by line with a doleful tune.
James Boswell once attended such a service, and thought it
quite the most dreadful sight in Edinburgh.

The Deacon still hoped for a reprieve; and many of his

* Their trial had taken place earlier in August.

Edinburgh friends did their best to move the Town Council
and Mr Pitt's right-hand man to action. To Henry Dundas,
Brodie wrote in manly terms asking for Botany Bay instead of
the Tolbooth gallows. He also wrote to the Duchess of Buccleuch – was there some old bond of kindness here? – putting
on the agony a little more, as he well might, September now
being half done.

My time flies apace, and the hand of Death presses upon me. Think
for one moment, but no longer, what it is to be wretched, doomed
to Death, helpless and in chains, and you will excuse an effort for
life from the most infatuated and miserable of men.

The letter was subscribed 'Edinr Tolbooth in the Iron Room
and in Chains'.

If gaming was not the reason for the Deacon's downfall,
then, thought Creech, it must be loose women, such as Mistress
Watt of Libberton's Wynd. One suspects that he himself was
the gentleman of his narrative who called on Brodie the day
before the hanging.

On Tuesday morning, the day before his execution, a gentleman,
who was visiting him, occasionally remarked the fatal consequences
of being connected with bad women, and in how many instances it
had proved ruinous – *Yes* said Brodie. '*Tis women seduces all mankind*'.
The gentleman reproved this levity; but he sung out the song.

The song, of course, coming from *The Beggar's Opera*.

On the Tuesday evening, the 30th of September [Creech's narrative
continued], the Magistrates gave an order that none should be
admitted to him but clergymen, a report having prevailed, that
there was an intention of putting self-destruction in his power. But
of this order he complained, and declared that if poison was placed
on one hand, and a dagger at the other, he would refuse them
both – he would submit to the sentence of the laws of his country.
Late in the evening he was suddenly agitated by hearing some noise;
and turning to Smith, he said '*George, Do you know what noise this is,*'
'*No,*' said Smith – '*Then I'll tell you. It is the drawing out of the fatal
beam, on which you and I must suffer tomorrow – I know it well.*'

And so he should. As Deacon of the Wrights two years back he
had had a hand in its design.

So after eleven, he went to bed, and slept till four in the morning,
and continued in bed till near eight. At nine (Wednesday October 1)

he had his hair full dressed and powdered. Soon after, a clergyman entered, and offered to pray with him. He desired it might be as short as possible.

The sinner would not come to repentance; and he looked with amusement on Smith, great booby that he was, kow-towing to the ministers, letting them put together an abject confession which purported to come from his own hand, though the fellow could not write. This was not the Deacon's way: he downed porter and beefsteaks.

Out of delicacy, he having been a juror, Creech absented himself from the spectacle of the execution. But he would not be far away; and the report he put together was as good as first-hand.

At two o'clock the guard marched up, and surrounded the place of execution; and soon after the Captain on duty informed the Magistrates, in the Council Chambers that all was ready.

The Magistrates then put on their robes of office, with white gloves, and white staves, and followed by the clergymen in black gowns and bands, proceeded from the Council Chamber to the prison, attended by the proper officers. The Magistrates reached the scaffold about ten minutes after two.

The criminals were soon after brought out. Brodie, at the first view of the immense multitude of spectators, and the dreadful apparatus, said '*This is awful!*' – On passing a gentleman he asked how he did, and said he was glad to see him. The gentleman answered, he was sorry to see Mr Brodie in that situation. Brodie replied, '*It is fortune de la guerre*'.

Brodie had on a full suit of black, his hair dressed and powdered; Smith was dressed in white, with black trimming. They were assisted in their devotions by the Rev. Mr Hardie, one of the ministers of the city, the Rev. Mr Cleeve of the Episcopal, and Mr Hall of the Burgher persuasion. They spent some time in prayer with seeming fervency. Brodie knelt, laying a handkerchief under his knees.

It would not do to dangle from the gallows with dusty breeches. For this was the supreme gamble of his life. *Fortune de la guerre*, indeed; but the war was not yet over. Here as he bowed to the crowd below was the very crest of the wave. By comparison it had been mere bravado to spirit young Hay away from the Tolbooth ten years back, and the excitement of the blood and betting round Michael Henderson's cockpit was tame. Not even adding mixing spice of treachery to old friends with the criminal deeds of the Brodie gang came anywhere near this; not even the risk of having to kill. At the time it had seemed the height of daring to attack the revenues of Scotland there in Chessel's Court. But that was nothing to what was now to be attempted – to cheat the hangman in full view of forty thousand.

That very morning the Deacon had written from the Tolbooth to Lord Provost Grieve, the undistinguished City Father with a new house on Princes Street. 'None of my relatives can bear to be with me at my last moments', he said, so 'it will be some consolation in my last hour if some friends could take their place.' Could orders also be given that after the fatal moment his body should be given to them and by no means allowed to remain in gaol? 'This', he ended, 'is the last request of your most obedient, but most unfortunate, William Brodie.' It was a request which the Lord Provost immediately granted.

There was, of course, much more to it than this. A few days before, his friends, presumably his cronies of the Cape, desperate that Sir Lewd should not die, had enlisted the help of a French doctor then in town. This Monsieur Pierre Degravers who said he had been 'Professor of Anatomy and Physiology in the Royal Academy of Science' at Paris but was offering his services to all comers at the rate of half a crown a time, had visited the Deacon in the Tolbooth. Together they had concerted the plan. The day before the execution, again he visited the old prison, this time marking the Deacon's temples and arms with a pencil that he might know where to cut; and the Deacon's friends saw to it that the hangman was bribed to make no fuss about the collar of steel concealed under the Deacon's neckerchief and to give a short drop.

So when he mounted the scaffold that afternoon the Deacon was blithely confident that he would get out of this scrape as out of all those that had gone before, 'Baillie, I'll see you at the deid-chack yet'* he had said to Creech, grinning all the while, the last time they met. Nor in this was he altogether giving way to fantasy. Only a dozen years before, James Boswell had had to be dissuaded by his friends from attempting the bringing back to life in this fashion of one of his clients, a

---

* A chack is a snack. The deid-chack was the dinner the Provost and Council gave themselves at Cleriheugh's (at the town's expense) after a public hanging.

sheep-stealer, whom he felt had had a raw deal from the
judges. And the case of 'Half-hangit Maggie Dickson' was still
a folk memory. She had been hanged for child murder some
sixty years past. Her body was duly delivered to her relatives
for burial and they put it in a cart to take the corpse out of
town. But before the journey was half over the victim revived –
to live and bear more brats, they said.

It is with this knowledge – which Creech did not have at
the time – that his narrative of the hanging is to be read. The
halter was to be the Deacon's salvation.

When the devotions were over [Creech continued], the great bell
began to toll, at half minute pauses, which had an awful and solemn
effect. The criminals put on white caps, and Smith, whose behaviour
was highly penitent and resigned, slowly ascended the platform.
It is said Brodie tapped Smith on the shoulder, saying '*Go up,
George, you are first in hand*'. He was raised a few feet above the
scaffold, and placed immediately under the beam where the halters
were fixed; he was followed by Brodie, who mounted with alertness
and examined the dreadful apparatus with attention, particularly
the halter designed for himself, which he pulled with his hand.

The ruse was going to work. It couldn't fail. The gallows
was to be cheated. Perhaps there was a glance of understanding between Brodie and the hangman. Perhaps someone saw it
– his old adversary, Davie Laing, the Town Clerk-Depute? For
now came disaster.

It was found that the halter had been too much shortened [continues
Creech ignorant of what was really happening], and they were
obliged to be taken down to alter. During this dreadful interval,
Smith remained on the platform trembling, but Brodie stepped
briskly down to the scaffold, took off his night cap, and again
entered into conversation with his friends, till the ropes were
adjusted. He then sprung up again upon the platform but the rope
was still improperly placed, and he once more descended, showing
some little impatience, and observed, that the executioner was a
bungling fellow, and ought to be punished for his stupidity – but
that it did not much signify.

His 'little impatience' was admirable. The best laid plans were
going agley; hope was running out; it was not to be an ending
as in *The Beggar's Opera*. After all, Macheath was to hang.
But in these last minutes he contrived to live out the part,

making a joke at the expense of the hangman, who, scared out of his skin, was now readjusting the rope to a lethal length.

Having again ascended, he deliberately untied his cravat, buttoned up his waistcoat and coat, and helped the executioner to fix the rope; then pulling the night-cap over his face, he folded his arms, and placed himself in an attitude expressive of firmness and resolution. Smith, who, during the interruption, had been in fervent devotion, soon after the adjustment of the halters, let fall a handkerchief as a signal, and a few minutes before three the platform dropt, and they were launched into eternity. Thus ended the Life of William Brodie and of George Smith.

Nevertheless, the rest of the plan went into action. He was quickly cut down, and his body was given to two workmen from the Brodie yard who put it in a cart and drove it furiously down the steep slope of the Netherbow, then round the cobbles of the Grassmarket. In the workshop off the Cowgate the French quack was waiting, his lancet ready.

But neither the jolting nor the bleeding did the trick. The Deacon's neck was broken and he was buried quietly in the churchyard near George's Square. Or so they said.

Half the town had watched the hanging. It only remained for the *Courant* to have its last fling. *The Beggar's Opera*, it said, should be banned: it put ideas into the heads of weaker brethren. (This, surely was from the pen of Willie Creech; his other favourite remedy for the national degeneracy was the banning of novels.) On behalf of the Town Council, the day after the hanging, Bailie Creech to-be presented the University a new silver mace to replace the one the Deacon had stolen. The Bruce brothers of the North Bridge successfully agitated for a share of the compensation that was going from the sale of the Deacon's properties. But the big family house knew the Brodies no more. And in the Club register one of the Deacon's cronies of the Cape drew a hanged man against his name.

Within a week of the hanging, the second edition of Creech's *Trial of William Brodie and George Smith* was on sale, complete with appendix describing the last days. For frontispiece, Kay the caricaturist, then making something of a name for himself at his shop in the Parliament Close, had drawn a full length of the Deacon in his prison cell. For posterity, there he stands, black satin breeches and fancy waistcoat, cane and cocked hat. The face gives nothing away. Is is that of a thousand Edinburgh citizens before or since who in their time have combined the day's business with a seat on the Council. On a table lie a stack of cards, some gaming dice and a bunch of keys. The smoking chimney pots of Auld Reekie look through the barred windows of the Tolbooth.

Already another version of the trial was on sale. As friend and legal agent to John Clerk, and eyewitness to all that had passed in the twenty-one hours of to and fro in the Parliament House, Aeneas Morison had brought out his own account. This was a much fuller narrative which reported the trial, Mr Morison explained defensively, in the English fashion of direct speech. Creech had given scarcely anything of John Clerk's assault on the Bench and nothing of his impertinences to Braxfield. Morison gave a still severely abridged version of what took place in the small hours of that night in Parliament House. In Henry Dundas's Scotland an establishment man would, if need be, make free with the facts; and a young lawyer with his way to make would no doubt think twice before reporting *verbatim* the discomfiture of my Lord Justice Clerk. None the less the demand was great. Within weeks Creech was fighting against the appearance of pirated editions of his book.

Niggardly to John Clerk Creech's bestseller might be, but that young advocate had no cause for bitterness. The trial of Deacon Brodie had made his name. *He* was the pleader who would go to great lengths for his client. *He* was the one who would stand up to judges. With this reputation, business flowed to him, even though he was still staunch for his Whiggism. Until in his old age he was himself elevated to the Bench as Cockburn was to recall, he was the torment of judges,* and he made a fortune.

It was Erskine who suffered. His forebodings that mild government would not last were soon fulfilled. Nine months after the Deacon's departure the Bastille of Paris was stormed. Soon the glare of events in France was reflected in Britain,

* See Appendix 2.

changing the more easy-going eighties into the repressive rule of the nineties. Men of property and substance persuaded themselves that Jacobin principles threatened the established order here too. The preservation of party and public order all too easily became one and the same. Henry Dundas as Home Secretary conceived it his duty to save the country from mob rule (and the scaremongering kept the Tories in the saddle).

This was the decade of the sedition trials when, were Henry Cockburn to be believed, oppressive government used hand-picked juries and an overbearing Lord Braxfield for its own ends. It is for these years that the old gentleman is remembered: his aside to one of his jurymen, 'Come awa', Maister Horner, come awa', an' help us to hing ane o' thae damned scoondrels'; his 'Ah've never liket the French, but noo ah hate them', and the most celebrated passage of all at the trial of the reformer Gerald:

MR GERALD – My Lord, all great men have been reformers. Even our Saviour was one.
LORD JUSTICE CLERK – Muckle he made o' that. He was hingit.

Freedom of speech and thought were indeed repressed in the meanest ways. 'A country gentleman with any principle except devotion to Henry Dundas was viewed as a kind of monster,' said Cockburn. It even happened that the radically minded shopkeeper in need of an overdraft would get short shrift from the Bank of Scotland. On the other hand with the warm appro-bation of his fellow judges the Lord Justice Clerk was enforcing the general will and the law of the land. The times were un-certain. No one knew when the set order might not dissolve as it had done in France. One year the King's Birthday in Edinburgh was celebrated, not with drinking and dead cats, but by a mob breaking the windows of Lord-Advocate Dundas. Sensible men everywhere, from Mr Walter Scott, W.S., of George's Square to Ilay Campbell now become Lord President of the Court of Session, were glad of old Braxie's commanding presence on the Bench. Today we look askance at the way he contrived to confound law with politics in charging the sedition trial juries; but significantly Cockburn, who was his chief detractor in the next generation, cavils only at the harshness of the sentencing. To be sent to Botany Bay, for all that friends and family knew, was to be as good as dead. However, in

Robert Louis Stevenson's mighty phrase (more of R.L.S. in a little), the Lord Justice Clerk was simply going up the great bare staircase of his duty.

For Erskine, the crisis came in the January of 1796. That winter he had presided at a public meeting which deplored the continuing war with France. 'Jacobin' went up the shout from respectable Edinburgh, and for all the lustre Erskine had given to the Scottish Bar, little Dundas had him hunted out of the Deanship of the Faculty of Advocates.

More and more he took himself off to Almondell, his violin, and his garden. It was a bitter draught to swallow. *Otium cum diggin a-tattie* he called it, as was his way, making a joke of a bad situation. But it was a poor consolation. Something of the community sense of old Edinburgh had been broken, never quite to be put together again. Briefly, and not too successfully, he put on the Lord-Advocate's gown in 1807 when the wheel of fortune spun for a little while in his favour. But Scotland had wasted his unique gifts of leadership.

Yet what Erskine had said at the Deacon's trial was to have an immeasurable consequence. 'I have heard it said' – so he had spoken against the admissibility of Brown the Irish thug – 'that the King could make a peer, but that he could not make a gentleman. I am sure that he cannot make a rogue an honest man.' Down in Dumfriesshire, Robert Burns caught the echo of his words. Perhaps he had read the reports in the newspaper and Harry Erskine's speech had stuck in his mind. Perhaps, mindful of his old Edinburgh acquaintances, he had bought a copy of Willie Creech's book. However it happened, seven years later, by the poet's alchemy Erskine's words become:

> A prince can mak a belted knight
> A marquis, duke an a' that
> But an honest man's aboon his might
> Guide faith, he manna fa' that.

A verse which was to lead on to the battle cry of Scottish radicalism, this in turn to reverberate round the world.

> For a' that, and a' that
> Its comin' yet for a' that
> That man to man, the world o'er
> Shall brothers be for a' that.

Defeated liberals like Henry Erskine tend to build better than they know.

As the years passed, Edinburgh tried to forget the Deacon. Perhaps he had caused the Edinburgh establishment embarrassment enough. His life had been no advertisement for the now embattled, soon to be reformed, system of self-electing town councils. The reticence may simply have been the gentleness of manners in that still Scottish society. Even in the overcrowding of the old town, especially there, private grief was respected. There would be decent regard to the feelings of Miss Jeannie and Mistress Jamie in St James's Square; to the Deacon's brother, a barber in the Lawnmarket; and to a host of other Edinburgh people who had drunk, deliberated, gambled and wenched with him.

In all of Scott there is only one mention of him, and that oblique. This is in a note to *The Heart of Midlothian*, where Scott quotes Mr Groves of Bow Street, 'No mischief but a priest or a woman in it'. (But heaven knows what was lost when an officious female consigned to the flames the whole of Sir Walter's splendid correspondence with his closest friend.) There is however temptation to read into Scott's presentation thesis of 1792 on his becoming an advocate at least a consciousness of the Brodie trial. The thesis was on the unusual and lugubrious subject of the disposal of the corpses of executed criminals – and it was dedicated to Lord Braxfield! Braxfield, as has been mentioned, was a friend of Scott's father; but, even so, one wonders if young Walter was sailing near the wind.

Old Henry Mackenzie remembered. Writing in his private notebook sometime in the 1820s from his new house in Heriot Row he put down what he recalled of the Deacon. Mackenzie had been the literary emience of old Edinburgh, in the pecking order higher even than Willie Creech. But he was also of a Highland family at no great distance from Brodie Castle, and so his first recollection was that the Deacon had been sib to the Laird of Milntown. He remembered too how important the Deacon had made himself at the disputed election of Sir Laurence Dundas, and what a stir he had caused in the town. As to the crimes of the Brodie gang he noted the general belief that they had on one occasion killed in the course of a robbery

(there is no record of this but Edinburgh memories are long).
Mackenzie had teased out the whole story of the attempt to
cheat the gallows and got much nearer than Willie Creech
ever did to understanding the Deacon. His, he said, was a
'heroism of villainy'. 'There is', he continued, 'a strange
profligate sort of pleasure in villainy for its own sake, like the
deep play of a whist player who enjoys his superiority over his
fellows.' It was close to the mark.

In his shop in the Parliament Close, Kay the caricaturist
remembered; and he delighted or embarrassed his public with
further drawings of Brodie and his associates. A mild, quiet
man, Kay was intrigued by the Deacon's strange personality;
even in a drawing he made of a contest in Henderson's cockpit
he put in the Deacon amongst the crowd, the long Brodie nose
and the big scar under his left eye.

When young Robert Chambers was writing his *Traditions of
Edinburgh* about the year 1820 he too was curious about Brodie
and he visited the big house down Brodie's Close. 'Brodie's
house', he wrote, 'is to be found in its original state, first door
up a turnpike stair in the south east corner of a small court
near the foot of the close. The outer door is remarkable for its
curious elaborate workmanship. The house is well built, and
the rooms exhibit some decorations of taste.' The house, said
Chambers, was occupied by one William Christie, 'a decent
carpenter'. A linen draper in the Lawnmarket occupied the
flat above 'once the abode of Miss Grace Barclay, who kept
a boarding school for young ladies'. (Had they been there
when Sir Lewd was in his prime?) Another wright and upholsterer possessed the workshop and yard. 'To this yard',
Chambers continues, 'it is said his body was conveyed, immediately on being cut down by his workmen, who were instructed
to use all their endeavours to procure reanimation – which they
did, it is also affirmed by some *with* effect.'

But these were reports which it would be difficult to authenti-
cate, said Chambers running away fast from his conjecture,
though it looks as if he knew more than he wrote. And yet,
years later there were rumours that people who knew him had
seen the Deacon in Paris but had prudently kept quiet about it;
and that when the burial site in the graveyard off Buccleuch
Place was opened an empty coffin was found. So the pleasing
thought can be entertained that there may have been a

Scotsman with a stiff neck making his living through the revolutionary years with a cabinet-maker of the Rue Antoine. Perhaps there is some faint confirmation of this in that from the big Brodie family bible all mention of the Deacon was deliberately removed. For whatever reason Miss Jeannie felt it necessary to pretend that her brother had never been.

Yet this is fantasy. It would be simply the shame of it all that made Miss Jeannie apply her scissors to the family bible. It is not to be thought that the Deacon could have kept quiet for evermore had he in fact escaped from the gallows. William Brodie would somehow have trumpeted his survival.

Then in the winter of 1824, the heart of Brodie's Edinburgh was destroyed. The gloom of that November night was first lit by fire licking out of the high tenement at the head of Old Assembly Close. From the narrow wynds of Old Edinburgh still not wholly given up to neerdoweels and pauper Irish a great crowd gathered to watch; nothing like a good blaze. The fire-fighters were slow to bring their pumps into action: and within an hour all six storeys fronting the cobbles of the High Street were a mass of flames.

The watching crowd knew what must happen next. Little more than the width of a handshake separated the blazing building from its neighbour on the other side of the Close. Fanned by the night wind the fire from its gaping windows must spread, and the engines would not be able to go down the narrow wynd. Some brave fellows got on to the roof of the high tenement and called to the firemen to give them a hose. But it could not be done and the building was soon alight.

Next to be consumed was the venerable office of the *Courant*. The crowd was more concerned with the hundreds of families, wailing women and excited children, now to be made homeless. Though the wind had dropped, it had done its work. The fire would not now be stopped.

Long afterwards it was the roar of the blaze people remembered; this, and how the sparks shot upwards as from a volcano, to descend in a snowstorm of ash. A lurid red tinged the clouds as the conflagration spread up the High Street towards the gothic walls of St Giles, down to the Tron, backwards to the ravine of the Cowgate. Watchers from the eyries of the tall

buildings all around saw the glare, reflected from the battle-
ments of the castle right round to the crags that soar above the
Palace of Holyroodhouse. Scores of Auld Reekie's chimneys
long unswept and set alight by the falling sparks, made it
seem that the whole town was on fire.

When morning came the Tron Kirk was seen to be alight.
Its familiar Dutch steeple stood little chance of survival, for a
timber structure underlay its sheath of lead, and by now the
whole was a fiery glow. Soon the lead of the roof was pouring
over the stonework in a molten stream, and the great bell
crashed among the blazing pews below. With this calamity,
the fire seemed halted, the raging beast sated; among the high
lands running down from the High Street to the Cowgate the
destruction was awful, but contained. Not so: the fire had
further yet to go. When night came it had broken out again
nearly half a mile away. This time it was the attic of an eleven-
storey tenement near the Parliament Close which was seen to
be alight. Soon the great tall building which looked across the
oblong piazza of the Close to the crown of St Giles's steeple
was ablaze.

As the fire in the Parliament Close roared away through the
morning of the second day, the exhausted firemen had a
kenspeckle reinforcement. To save the courts, advocate and
judge, lawyer's clerk and my Lord Justice Clerk set themselves
to the pumps. As befitted the government's chief law officer,
the Lord-Advocate worked harder than any. To cries of 'Weel
dune, my Lord', he hosed the house where he had been born.
In the frenzy of fire-fighting all distinctions of rank were laid
aside. The hail and gusty showers of rain were unheeded; and
though the Parliament Close was lost, the Parliament House
was saved. Now the blaze was kept to the crevasse-like wynds,
and there it burned itself out, the blackened gaping buildings
round the Close threatening every moment to fall in a heap.
With iron cables, chains and ropes above and explosives below,
forty bluejackets from H.M.S. *Brisk* in Leith Roads brought
the great mass safely to the ground. It was the end of Brodie's
Edinburgh.

By now the old Tolbooth had also been taken down; with that
was lost the figure of a draught board which the Deacon had
contrived to cut out on the stone floor of the Iron Room.
Here (Chambers again the authority) the memory of him was

that 'he amused himself playing with anyone who would join him; and in default of such with his right hand against his left'. A split mind to the end.

Old Edinburgh was fast becoming the vilest slum in Europe: the city of Brodie and Harry Erskine, that of Burke and Hare.

By the 1850s, the corpse of the old town looked down from its windy ridge on a Princes Street which had already lost something of its tone. Along the noble thoroughfare, shopkeepers were knocking out the fronts of the demure grey houses. But then, as the spread of the railways ended the winter isolation of Highland castle and country seat, upper-class Edinburgh generally was losing its leavening of the Scotch nobility. Edinburgh was now in the throes of the second Reformation which had set up the Free Kirk of Scotland in evangelical opposition to the wealthy Established Church.

> The Free Kirk, the wee Kirk, the Kirk withoot the steeple,
> The Auld Kirk, the cauld Kirk, the Kirk withoot the people.

The kirks, not the clubs, were now the centres of social life. The Cape was no more; and the last sedan chair had vanished from the streets, though it would have been possible, just ten years past, to be carried by chair to the new Haymarket Station for a railway journey to Glasgow.

For the professional upper class, a fashionable place to live was now Heriot Row, where the second New Town of Edinburgh sloped down to the Water of Leith. Its generous face was turned to the sun. Across the street were ornamental and wholly private gardens. Here, newly established at No. 17, was the sedate residence of Mr Thomas Stevenson who built lighthouses in the Hebrides. And it was by means of the household of this rather heroic civil engineer that Deacon Brodie took on his improbable immortality.

Two agents within the house were at work. One was a piece of furniture standing in the bedroom of Mr Stevenson's frail little son. On his conviction the Deacon's property had passed to the Crown. Perhaps it was at the sale subsequently of the Deacon's effects that young Louis Stevenson's great-grandfather, then a well-doing manufacturer of lamps and lanterns in the

town, had bought a big mahogany cabinet* of sound craftsmanship and handsome appearance. However it had come into
the family, the tradition was clear; Deacon Brodie had made it.
Second was the nursemaid, become trusted family retainer.
She was from the country but to the delicate youngster she
was a great retailer of the stories of old Edinburgh, true or
fanciful, grim or ghostly. It was through her, the revered
'Cummy', that Louis met the Deacon, the Brodie handiwork
in the corner ever a reminder that once he had been more
than a ghostly being.

To Edinburgh working folk the Deacon had now taken on
something of a supernatural aura, like Major Weir who had
made a compact with the Devil and haunted the West Bow
for the past century and a half. In a way Brodie stood for the
half memory of the vibrant life of the old town, now given over
to drunks, their doxies and the very poor. The legends reflected
this. The threat there had been to the shopkeepers from the
highly organized workings of the Brodie gang had no part in
these. They were simply of Brodie the mystery man who had
flitted at will in and out of private houses.

There was the story – but was it a legend, or was it true? –
of the lady in a house not far from Brodie's Close, indisposed
and so unable to sail forth to church one Sunday in the 1780s.
Sitting alone in the house, for her servant had no such excuse
to absent herself from divine worship, she was astonished to
see a man come into the room, a crape over his face. He saw
her; not at all deterred he took up the keys lying on the table,
opened her bureau and coolly took out a large sum of money
which had been locked there. He touched nothing else, but
deliberately relocked the drawer, replaced the keys on the
table, made a low bow and retired. Fright kept her silent
throughout the bizarre performance, but she was sure she
recognized the intruder. Beyond a doubt it was Deacon Brodie;
and yet it *couldn't* be him. And so she kept it to herself.

Then there was the Deacon's friend who had happened to
mention to him that he would be away from home for some
days. But affairs detained the good burgess in town, and he
was in his own bed, as it happened unable to sleep (the Welsh
rabbits and Glasgow herring of a Cape supper?), when he

*To be found now in the Stevenson Museum, Lady Stair's House,
Edinburgh.

heard a noise in the next room. So he crept out of bed and climbed up to a false window to peer into the neighbouring room. There, a dark lantern in his hand, was his friend the Deacon. In this story, as in the previous one, the victim did nothing about it. As they would say, the Deacon was at his frolic.

Then, since there was nothing the Edinburgh working class treasured so much as a story with a dog in it, there was the marvellous coincidence which had led to George Smith being lodged in the Tolbooth, and through him to the unmasking of the Brodie gang. That March morning, when the Cowgate grocer was first hauled up the hill to the Sheriff-Clerk's Office, the farm-hand at Duddingston who had seen the theft of the plough-coulter used at Chessel's Court had not been able to identify Smith. But he said he did remember a big black dog the thieves had with them. At that very moment – so went the story – there was a scratching at the Sheriff-Clerk's door and George Smith's black Labrador burst in, wagging his tail at having found his master.*

'Thon's the verra dug,' said the farm-hand, better at identifying animals than people. And poor Smith's card house of denials collapsed.

Perhaps the stories of Brodie's success in cheating the gallows, of the empty coffin in the churchyard near George's Square, are to be considered of this genre. But common to them all was the vision of Brodie the will o' the wisp, Macheath–Brodie, the Deacon as he saw himself; and the stories lodged in young Louis Stevenson's mind as he progressed through his precocious childhood.

By the late 1860s he was a youth grown into rebellion against the churchy life of Heriot Row. The 'brawling Sabbath bells', as St Andrew's answered St Stephen's, and St George's of the Free Kirk chided St George's of the Established Church, were too much for the perceptive and romantic view of life he was already forming. It was in this state of revolt from his class and background that he became aware of the brothels and the huddle of dram shops less than half a mile from Heriot Row, only a step away from the east end of Princes Street. Young Louis was quickly fascinated by this quarter which had once

---

* This explains the dog's head in the corner of Kay's portrait 'The first meeting of Deacon Brodie and George Smith'.

been Mistress Jamie's genteel home and where the remnants of respectability were now embattled by the general squalor. For long afterwards the whispered Edinburgh tradition was that there he ruined his health. For a time he was said to have been in love with a loose girl from one of the local establishments. Fifty years later a biographer from across the Atlantic said that the girl's name and much else besides had been divulged to him by those who remembered R.L.S.'s unhappy years. (This belated presentation of 'Kate Drummond', Stevenson's dark-haired *amourette*, and her successors sparked off a furore in an Edinburgh nurtured on *Treasure Island*. Since then Furnas's biography has dispelled some of this conjecture. But even he conceded that there was such a girl; and in these years undergraduate Stevenson wrote as if he had indeed dropped out of the world of Heriot Row.

> I love night in the city,
> The lighted streets and the swinging gait of harlots.

And yet before each nocturnal foray, at five o'clock when the New Town moved to the dinner table young Louis would be in company with his gentle and charitable parents – though they drew the line at Kate.

Some Stevenson biographers have made light of this unhappy period in his life. Not so those familiar with the confusion a young Scotsman of gentle and pious upbringing would feel on his first encounter with the wickedness of the world. It has also to be underlined that the Calton Hill was not Montparnasse. He was minglng not with an artistic Bohemia, but with Scotch squalor at its worst; and the experience must have seared him. Edinburgh too has chosen to forget this unattractive part of its history, but it happens that the Court of Session records expose the life of this quarter in the very years of Stevenson's apostasy from Church and family. *Robertson v Steuart* as reversed in the House of Lords by *Steuart v Robertson* is the ghost that will not go away.*

That *cause célèbre* deserves a moment's disgression. It was about the disputed marriage of the son and heir to Sir William Drummond Steuart of Grandtully Castle in Strathtay. Major Steuart was a gallant fellow but had come a cropper. Sword

* Cases decided in the Court of Session, Court of Justiciary and the House of Lords: 1873–4 1R 532; 1875 2R (HL) 80.

in hand he had stood in the Thin Red Line at Balaclava; with the same immortal 93rd he had won a Victoria Cross in the Indian Mutiny; then he had gone on half-pay and had taken to drink and the steaming life near the east end of Princes Street. The upshot was a Scots marriage 'by habit and repute' with a girl from his Leith Street lodgings. The Major went to an early grave and in the Courts a bitter battle followed. Should the family's vast Perthshire estates be allowed to pass to the infant product of this none too regular union? Counsel for the Steuart family could only succeed in preventing this by exposure for what it was of the *faubourg* of the Major's final degradation. So Edinburgh learned more than it wished to know; and there was preserved to history a lurid picture of this quarter which the good and godly shunned and young Louis Stevenson frequented.

Close by was Stevenson's favourite pub of these early years, Rutherford's at the head of Leith Street, midway on the student axis between Old College and the New Theatre Royal. (It still stands, a grey ghost of a building, awaiting demolition.) There he must have rubbed shoulders with Major Steuart; and in his admirable little book on Edinburgh, blandly entitled 'Edinburgh: Picturesque Notes', Stevenson has left a deep-felt picture of the well-born drunkard which could be the Major to the life. Indeed, we know too much of this Edinburgh, and of Stevenson's dabbling in it, to write off these years as his 'chimes at midnight' period. Years later, in retrospect, he was also to recall desolating misery in its 'vicious, lamp lit, fairyland'. The double lives he observed in the district's clientele; the double part forced on himself as his yearning for Kate, or whomever, pulled against parental love; arguably, their awfulness never left him. (Twenty years later – in memory of Kate? – he named the solitary heroine of his novels *Catriona Drummond*. Pronounce her name, as one should, *Catri"na*.)

Meanwhile, from youth onwards, Deacon Brodie had featured in Stevenson's literary ambitions. There has been an adolescent attempt at a play, which has not survived. As he left Leith Street behind, became an advocate of sorts and shaped a writer's course, his fascination with the tale intensified. The very first of his myriad biographers, Miss Eve Simpson of the New Town set of these later Edinburgh days, recalled an evening in the mid-seventies when Stevenson allowed his imagination to range from Deacon Brodie to the nature of evil.

At this time he had much of his future work simmering in his brain. One evening he broke out into a species of Jekyll and Hyde plot. Deacon Brodie, the hypocritical villain, who appeared as a pillar of the Church (sic.), and an able craftsman before his fellow-townsmen, and was really a gambler and a burglar, suggested to Tusitala the two-sidedness of human character, 'commingled out of good and evel', the smug front to the world, the villain behind the mask.

In her rather breathless style Miss Simpson, an old Flame of R.L.S., put down her other memories, flowing from that evening a score of years past. In response to his thoughts on the nature of evil the others present called Stevenson a fraud in that his agreeable little magazine pieces gave no hint of his own darker side. This nettled him.

He avoided their company for some weeks, and laboured sedulously at a novel which would out-Herod Herod. He laid it before them, and they were startled with its strength, its terribleness, its out-rageous blackness of human depravity.

The Deacon was indeed emerging from his coffin.

This novel, curiously titled *History of Mexico*, remained in manuscript and has been lost. But the Deacon was still in Stevenson's mind. When, in 1878, he gored conformist Auld Reekie with his *Picturesque Notes* he retold with verve the legends of the Deacon. But, significantly, he did not delve to unearth the historical Deacon, though in the Advocate's Library the narratives of the trial would have been his for the asking. Rather he read into the legends his own interpretation. Re-telling Brodie's nocturnal invasions of private houses in the tall lands, he wrote: 'Still, in the mind's eye, he may be seen, a man harassed below a mountain of duplicity slinking from a magistrate's supper room to a thieves' den, and pickeering among the closes by the flicker of a dark lamp.'

'Harassed below a mountain of duplicity' is hardly a sum-ming up of the man who would play at draughts while the hammering of the gallows into the Tolbooth wall resounded through the Iron Room. Stevenson was beginning to exercise the privilege of every great imaginative writer: history was now his trampoline. The Deacon's story was the means by which he had begun to crystallize his thoughts on the manyness of man.

Not surprisingly, his next literary enterprise was to take up his adolescent play, and transform it into melodrama for the London stage. 'The great drammy of *Deacon Brodie, or the Two Lives* nears an end' he wrote from the Savile Club to his lawyer crony Charles Baxter in November 1878. There, and at the Stevenson family house on the slopes of the Pentland Hills, work went on on successive drafts through the early months of 1879, his big red-headed friend W. E. Henley collaborating. They had high hopes of their efforts. Why not the great Irving for the title role? 'Shall we find anyone to play it? Echo is fondly hoped to echo Irvine (sic). We are as modest as that. But it's all in the hands of the Right Honourable Member for Heaven.'

In *Deacon Brodie or the Double Life* as he completed it, Smith the flashy Englishman, John Brown alias Humphrey Moore the Irish bruiser, Ainslie the Scotch thief, and Jeannie Watt the Edinburgh tart are all deftly presented. But the action is compressed into the space of two days; the Deacon despatches the deplorable Ainslie; and in turn the last act sees him conveniently fall to the sword of a Bow Street runner.

In brief, the piece is a travesty of the Brodie story, and it also failed as theatre. The subject cries out for Stevenson the historical novelist, a role he had not yet found for himself; and the conventions of Victorian melodrama, its five acts and eight tableaux, proved too tight-laced a corset. But there are a couple of passages which adumbrate stretches of his inspired vision of the next decade, *The Strange Case of Dr Jekyll and Mr Hyde*; the Deacon, like Jekyll, is given a conscience; and Moore, the Irish thug, dominates him as Hyde was to rule the good Doctor. What is more, *why* Stevenson failed with *Deacon Brodie or the Double Life* and succeeded with *Jekyll and Hyde* is illuminating. In the play avarice and addiction to gambling are the motives, afflictions unknown to Stevenson, too generous for the one, too imaginative for the other. Try as he might, he could not write of them with conviction. But in the novel the kind of double life he described was rooted in an area of experience and observation of which the younger Stevenson had searing memories.

The most important stepping stone of all towards *Jekyll and*

Hyde was perhaps the very fact of the play's failure in London. It had been badly received in Glasgow; it had toured the States with some success; now in London it lived briefly in 1884. Henry Irving did not portray the Deacon. The play was soon on its way to limbo. But its theme matured in Stevenson's mind.

Two years later, it was in a drugged sleep, Stevenson was to say, that the vision came to his bedside of Jekyll the moral man who must become the bestial Hyde. 'All I dreamed of Dr Jekyll', he wrote, 'was that one man was being pressed into a cabinet when he swallowed a drug and changed into another.' The cabinet,* as has been conjectured, was perhaps a hazy memory of the old piece of furniture of the Deacon's craftsmanship which stood in the corner of his room at Heriot Row. Who can say what it had meant to the precocious and impressionable youngster in those midnight terrors that did not find their expression in *The Child's Garden of Verses*?

The matter of the Deacon's cabinet perhaps has only the importance of a footnote. What is germane to tracing the descent from Brodie to Jekyll is that Stevenson's novel has so much of Edinburgh in it. G. K. Chesterton first made this point. Though ostensibly the setting is London, Edinburgh of the windy gaslit streets and forbidding tenements was much in Stevenson's mind.

The fog is a London fog; but Utterson, the dry lawyer round whom the story revolves, is so clearly a solicitor of the old school (the breed is not yet quite extinct) and an Edinburgh man; Jekyll a Scots physician made good. It is, I think, possible to go further than this and assert that Stevenson, master as always of the topographical novel, had specifically in mind the faded quarter of his undergraduate revolt when he wrote of Jekyll's place of residence. Henry Jekyll's house is in 'a square of ancient, handsome houses, now for the most part decayed from their high estate and let in flats and chambers to all sorts and conditions of men; map-engravers, architects, shady lawyers, and the agents of obscure enterprises'. It backs on to a small disreputable street – this an Edinburgh, not a

---

* In *Dr Jekyll and Mr Hyde* Stevenson uses a French word for Jekyll's chamber of horrors: it is his *cabinet*. This could be a play on words, the Deacon's 'cabinet' still in his mind as he wrote the novel in the course of six frenzied days.

London, characteristic. The sinister building on this back street through which Hyde makes his way to Jekyll's house after his night-time adventures ('. . . the door which was equipped with neither bell nor knocker was blistered and distained. Tramps slouched into the recess and struck matches on the panels; children kept shop upon the steps . . .') could have been any one of the down-at-heel thoroughfares off the east end of Princes Street.

Consider the Edinburgh of these years. By Stevenson's day the Old Town was hopelessly engulfed in the general slum. It was over a quarter of a century since the last judge had lived there (old Lord Glenlee, who to the very end walked fully robed, hat in hand through the evil ghetto to Parliament House). The other squares, terraces, rows and crescents of the New Town presented a schiltrom of respectability to encircling, industrial Edinburgh. Some streets had a bad name: Rose Street of the pubs, Cumberland Street with its drunken fights and wife-beatings. But only at the eastern edge, the earliest part of the New Town, did the remnants of gentility continue to live cheek by jowl with urban squalor. One word in the novel may be taken to give the final confirmation. To reach the square in which stood Jekyll's house, old Utterson the lawyer had to 'mount' a little street. Their sleaziness apart, all the streets of this quarter had this in common: they were steep.

Within his big house in the shabby square, a different kind of double life to that of the Deacon in the melodrama was practised by the esteemed and kindly bachelor, Dr Henry Jekyll. Lechery not avarice was the propellant; he had an inclination towards the style of life which the Victorian upper class considered loose. More conveniently to indulge these appetites, while losing nothing of his respectable standing in society, he found the means of changing miraculously into the hedonist Edward Hyde; Hyde the slave in turn becoming a macabre figure, wholly degraded by his pleasures and the absolute ruler of his 'master'. Disguise it as he might – and the novel, conceived by Stevenson as a 'shilling shocker' to please the publishers and pay his bills, had to be as acceptable in the drawing room as in the smoking room – the theme was sadistic lust. It is about the war of the members, said Jekyll himself. He could not have put it plainer than that.

'The pleasures which I made haste to seek in my disguise were undignified', so ran Jekyll's confession when he understood that, Faustus-like, he had sold his soul to his own private devil. 'I would scarce use a harder term. But in the hands of Edward Hyde they soon began to turn towards the monstrous. When I would come back from these excursions, I was often plunged into a kind of wonder at my vicarious depravity.' The ladies would wonder, but some gentlemen would know only too well the meaning behind these words, just as they would recognize what went on in the street of Hyde's lodgings, 'a dingy street, a gin palace, a low French eating house, a shop for the retailing of penny numbers and twopenny salads, many ragged children huddled in the doorways, and many women of different nationalities passing out, key in hand'. The reader's first encounter with Hyde is his collision in a night-time street with a child, and his trampling over her. The incident has a contrived look about it; but its significance is that it stands for all that the Edward Hydes inflicted on the poor sluts of Victorian society.

The seeming moral is clear, if un-Stevensonian: let cutty sarks run in your mind and like the good Dr Jekyll you may come to this. Hence the novel's *succès fou*, its fabulous sales on both sides of the Atlantic, and the commendation it was given from the pulpit of St Paul's Cathedral. But Henry Jekyll's fatal attribute is not his taste for low pleasure. It is his ability to disintegrate his personality. If one may so respectfully suggest to the shades of a hundred Victorian critics the retribution that follows hypocrisy is the real theme.

Whether Stevenson was impelled to this theme by the intensity of the war that had been within himself or whether in his years of youthful debauchery he had taken note of some respected Edinburgh hypocrite who systematically split his day between a New Town and a Leith Street brothel is a teasing question. Our concern here is rather the ancestry of Jekyll, of whose hypocrisy one can only say – how very different it all was from the night-life of Deacon Brodie! We may be tolerably certain that Sir Lewd in his dignity as Deacon of the Wrights made his way down Libberton's Wynd to Jeannie Watt's (and in his time down other Edinburgh closes to her many predecessors) free of any need to pretend that he was on some civic errand. But then, in matters of overt morality, Edinburgh

of the Golden Jubilee differed from Edinburgh of the Golden
Age in this, that Willie Creech had won at last.

If then his literary after-life had turned Brodie the rogue into
Jekyll the hypocrite, there remains a deep-down similarity
between the two. Stevenson's novel is a mighty step forward in
literature in that it bares the roots of evil; and in one important way these were common to the douce Doctor and his
eighteenth-century ancestor. Evil, Stevenson is saying, is not
necessarily resorted to with reluctance and a shamed face.
It can be taken to hungrily, and with a sense of glory. Slipping
into the guise of Edward Hyde, freeing himself from the bonds
of decency, Henry Jekyll knows a great sense of release.

I felt younger, lighter, happier in body; within I was conscious of a
heady recklessness, a current of disordered sensual images running
like a mill-race in my fancy, a solution of the bonds of obligation,
an unknown but not an innocent freedom of the soul. I knew
myself, at the first breath of this new life, to be more wicked,
tenfold more wicked, sold a slave to my original evil; and the
thought, in that moment, braced and delighted me like wine.

There is the Deacon. He needs no plinth in Princes Street
Gardens for memorial.

Climbing the steep pavement of the street from the Grassmarket to the George IV Bridge you pass where the turnpike
stair that led to Deacon Brodie's house once stood. Not far
away, and opposite the entry to Brodie's Close – the very
opening through which he would come on to the High Street
every morning, cane, cocked hat, and a curious way of walking
– is a pub that bears his name. In Parliament House the old
Justiciary Court is now the advocates' robing room, all traces
of its former role effaced, and in the library the case of Brodie
and Smith is itself only a mention in a footnote to the dissertation on the exercise of the Royal Prerogative of Mercy in
Alison on Crimes. Further down the High Street another tavern
keeps the memory of its lineal descent from the evil little house
where the Deacon gambled the night and his winnings away.
In Chessel's Court by an inspired piece of preservation, the
buildings are still in their eighteenth-century guise; what was
once the General Excise Office of Scotland looks today much
as it did on the March evening of the bungled break-in of

E*

nearly two hundred years ago. Further down the Canongate, in Huntly House you see the letter he wrote from the Tolbooth gaol as he awaited his trial and felt annoyance that no one could come to cut his fingernails.

If all this inclines you to be generously disposed you might try to make excuses for him; and the Bard's 'What's done we partly may compute / But know not what's resisted' might come to mind. Or you might conjecture that the new dimensions the Deacon gave to dishonesty was a sort of parody of Edinburgh's double ways in Kirk matters, and that dishonesty is indivisible.

But moralizing would be better left to the Willie Creeches who are always with us. Enough perhaps to reflect that but for the Deacon we would not have the Deacon's tale which brings on stage the heroes of old Edinburgh in its decades of greatness; Braxfield and Harry Erskine, John Clerk, Creech himself, Eskgrove, Ilay Campbell and the Dundases. The old town of Edinburgh is now all but gone; frayed at the edges and shorn of the glory of its rural setting the New Town survives, but only in its architecture. The talk, the debate, the clash of mind on mind in his lively society have all perished except as re-created for the space of a day and a night in the trial of William Brodie. For this we owe him a great debt.

Yet you *can* meet Brodie face to face if you go to the George IV Bridge in Edinburgh and call for the copy of Aeneas Morison's narrative of the trial, presented to the Advocates Library in 1919. There in the end papers you may read the Deacon's last will and testament, written on the morning he was hanged, possibly – say the experts – in his own hand.

That morning, as the hour of his execution stalked nearer and nearer, the Deacon would know for sure that there would be no last minute reprieve. Neither Henry Dundas nor the Duchess of Buccleuch had even passed on his letters to Lord Sydney, but from his castle near Forres Brodie of Brodie, swallowing his not inconsiderable pride, had brought himself to ask the Secretary of State that his kinsman's sentence be Botany Bay rather than the gallows. Not that there was any-thing to be said for the Deacon, the Laird of Brodie hastened to add; but the disgrace of a hanging would mortify the Brodie gentry whereas clemency would put them under a lasting obligation to the present administration. And on the petition a Home Office clerk had written, 'He has been told it cannot be done'.

So in the knowledge that there would be no reprieve, not knowing whether Degravers' ministrations would do the trick, he set to writing his will.

I William Brodie, late deacon of the wrights in Edinburgh [he wrote] and some time a member of the town council of the said city, considering the certainty of my death, and the propriety and expediency of recommending my memory to my friends when I am no more, do therefore hereby execute my last will and testament. Having a Royal successor to my means and estate, and nothing else to dispose of but my good and bad qualifications, I hereby dispose of them as follows.

First he set about the Lord Provost, due to demit office, but known to be on the look-out for a new post.

To the Right Honourable (for a few days to come) John Grieve Esqr. I bequeath my political knowledge in securing magistrates and packing corporations . . .

Now for his enemies, pride of place going to Donaldson, the pirating publisher who had sat in the Trial Jury.

To deacon James Donaldson I give and bequeath my good breeding and sobriety, which may prevent his being kicked out of company for his petulance and ill-manners, as was lately the case at Archer's Hall.

Archer's Hall, home of the Royal Company of Archers, then a focus of Edinburgh society. So, on to the Magistrates, with a side swipe at Jamie Laing, the Depute Town Clerk.

To the Magistrates of Edinburgh present and to come I leave and bequeath all my knowledge of the Law, that they may not be under the necessity in future of borrowing from either of the Jamies, their clerks who are as ignorant as themselves.

And to the Kirk

My charity and good deeds I humbly bequeath to the Ministers of the Church of Scotland with this injunction that they will not retail them among their hearers, but put them in practice themselves.

Willie Creech, of course, merited a paragraph on his own. He had posed as a friend and then prosed away about the iniquity of this misspent life.

To William Creech, Bookseller, who has favoured the public with an account of my trial, I give and grant my honour and gratitude . . .

But the strain of this gallows humour was telling, and the Deacon confused his words as he went on to refer to 'the note prefixed Morrison's Appendix in his edition' in which young Aeneas had boldly complained of Creech's conduct.

To Hamilton, the chimney sweeper [he continued, perhaps pulling himself together] I freely bequeath my dexterity at cards and dice, trusting when he gets a pigeon that it will enable him to refund himself of the money which he prosecuted me for, which I advertise him, he is not likely to do either at Clarke's or Michael Henderson's.

To my good friends and companions Brown and Ainslie I bequeath my villainy and whole other bad qualities, not doubting but their own will secure them a rope at last.

Now the hubbub of the assembling crowd would be heard through the high grated windows of the Iron Room, and so the Deacon came to his mock conclusion.

And lastly my neck being now about to be embraced by a halter I recommend to all Rogues, Sharpers, Thieves and Gamblers, as well in high as in low stations to take care of theirs by leaving of all wicked practices and becoming good members of society.

All this he subscribed with his flourishing signature and, as any will should be, dated it properly, 'October 1st 1788 – Edinburgh Tolbooth'.

Raeburn never painted his delinquent fellow member of the Cape. But here in his last Will and Testament is the jaunty portrait of himself which the Deacon wished to leave to posterity. He would have been glad to learn that he was claimed as an ancestor by the heroine of Muriel Spark's Edinburgh novel – Miss Jean *Brodie*.

The Sources

Pride of place must go to William Roughead's indispensable *Trial of Deacon Brodie* which put together the various accounts; Creech's, Morison's, and Peter Mackenzie's which is based on Morison's notes.

The question is, should Peter Mackenzie's account be accepted? Mackenzie was a journalist with a pleasant chatty style, and sometimes a free way with the truth. Oddly enough for this very Edinburgh story his version of the battle between John Clerk and the Bench appeared in his *Reminiscences of Glasgow*, which he brought out in the 1860s. To arrive at a view of the credibility of Mackenzie, first set his version alongside Creech's report of the relevant part of John Clerk's address to the jury. Here is Creech.

The evidence, so far as regarded Smith, was two-fold. In the first place, the parole testimony of the witnesses, adduced for the prosecutor, and the relative circumstances; and secondly, the supposed real evidence arising from his own declarations.

With regard to the first of these, Mr Clerk was proceeding to state to the Jury, that he would be able to show, that evidence had been admitted in this case, which was both *improper* and *inadmissible*; the Lord Justice Clerk, however, interrupted him and said, as the Court had determined the admissibility of the whole evidence led, it was reflecting upon the judgment of the Court now to call it in question. Mr Clerk, however, insisted, that he was not then under the correction of the Court. That he was addressing himself to the Jury, who were judges both of the law and of the fact.

After some farther altercation on this head, it was agreed, that as the Dean of Faculty would have occasion to occupy that ground, and to state the import of the parole testimony to the Jury, it would be altogether unnecessary to anticipate what he had to say on that head. Mr Clerk then proceeded.

That this is an amputation of the truth is clear from Aeneas Morison's account, published within a few days of Creech's.

It hints at a great deal more having been said. Here is how he reports John Clerk.

I come next to the testimony of Ainslie and Brown. Gentlemen, you have heard a variety of objections stated to the admissibility of their evidence; all of which have been over-ruled by the Court. But notwithstanding judgment of their Lordships, I must here adhere to these objections, and maintain that they ought not to have been admitted as witnesses.

LORD JUSTICE CLERK – Do you say that, Sir, after the judgment which the Court has pronounced?

MR CLERK – My Lord, I know that your Lordships have determined this question; but the jury have not. They are judges both of the fact and of the law; and are not bound by your Lordships determination, unless it agrees with their own opinion. Unless I am allowed to speak to the jury in this manner, I am determined not to speak a word more. I am willing to sit down if your Lordships command me. (Here Mr Clerk sat down.)

LORD JUSTICE CLERK – This is most indecent behaviour. You cannot be allowed to speak to the admissibility; to the credibility you may.

MR CLERK – This has been too often repeated. I have met with no politeness from the Court. I have been snubbed rather too often, my Lord, I maintain that the jury are judges of the law as well as of the fact; and I am positively resolved, that I will proceed no further, unless I am allowed to speak in my own way.

LORD HAILES – You had better go on, Mr Clerk. Do go on.

DEAN OF FACULTY – If it will satisfy Mr Clerk: I can assure him, that I will plead on this point to the jury, waving all objection to the admissibility, which it may be rather irregular to plead after the decision of the Court.

LORD JUSTICE CLERK – Dean of Faculty, I know you will attempt nothing that is improper.

MR CLERK – I say, Gentlemen, I adhere to all the objections stated on the proof, both to the admissibility and to the credibility of these witnesses. On the other and, it is obvious, that if they are to be listened as to good and unexceptionable witnesses, their evidence goes to prove the guilt of my client in the clearest and most unequivocal manner; so that the question comes to be. How far are they admissible at all? And how far are they credible? Is their evidence to be laid aside altogether? And if not, to what extent is it worthy of belief? Gentlemen, before I was interrupted, I was going to observe, that in this branch of the evidence my cause is the same with that which is to be supported with so much greater abilities by the Dean of Faculty; and of consequence it would be unnecessary and even impertinent in me to take up your time in arguing at large upon the subject.

It is with these that Peter Mackenzie's version has to be contrasted. That version, as adopted by Roughhead, and changed only to the extent of giving back to Braxfield and Clerk their Scotch accents, is the one I have used. But MacKenzie's introduction must give the historian some qualms.

The marvellous story we are now about to relate to our readers occurred in the year 1788, that is, nearly eight years ago, before we were born. Of course we can tell nothing about it from personal knowledge at the time, but one of the agents of one of the prisoners intimately connected with it was the late Aeneas Morison, Esq., grandfather of the present Mr Arch Robertson, manager of the Royal Bank in Glasgow. He used often to tell us the story in our younger days, more than forty years ago. It made a very vivid impression on us at the time, not yet effaced. Mr Morison was pleased to present us in the year 1816 with a pamphlet published about it by Mr William Creech of Edinburgh, long previous to that date; but he stated to us this fact, that the pamphlet did not contain anything about, but purposely concealed for fear of offending the judges, a most interesting scene in the Justiciary Court between the famous John Clerk, Esq, of Eldon, advocate, and the equally famous Lord Justice Clerk Braxfield. It was Mr Clerk's first or earliest appearance in any case of importance in the Justiciary Court. It was 'the making of him' at the Bar, at his first clerk and friend, Mr Morrison, used to observe; and with the original notes on that pamphlet, given to us as we have just stated, by Mr Morrison himself in the year 1816, we are enabled to brush up our memory pretty accurately we think, with what follows, which may amuse or divert some of our readers; and if we neglected the opportunity, the occasion might die with ourselves.

Though sometimes they can give revealing glimpses, in this instance the Books of Adjournal of the High Court of Justiciary are of no help one way or the other. The record of the trial follows the usual form; it details the wording of the indictment, and the Defence counsel's objections to its adequacy both in the description of Brodie's effects and in its failure to distinguish which of the offices in Chessel's Court was the scene of the crime. The witnesses are listed but there is nothing of their evidence nor of their examination. The argument before the Bench as to the admissibility of Ainslie and Brown is summarized, and the judge's decision recorded, as was necessary for this the 'memory' of the High Court of Justiciary. But all that happened between midnight and six o'clock on the 28th of August is compressed into the following.

The following witnesses were adduced in excuplation of the pannell William Brodie.

1 Mathew Sheriff, upholsterer in Edinburgh
2 Jane Watt, residenter in Edinburgh
3 Peggy Giles, servant to George Graham, publican at Muttonhole near Edinburgh
4 Helen Alison, spouse to William Wallace, mason in Edinburgh
5 James Murray, a former deponent
6 James Laing, a former deponent
7 Robert Smith, a former deponent

The prosecutors for the pannell Brodie declared that they closed their evidence in exculpation and the prosecutors for the pannell George Smith declared that they had no evidence to adduce in exculpation.

The evidence was then summed up, upon the part of the prose-cutor by His Majesty's Advocate, on the part of the pannell William Brodie by Mr Henry Erskine, on the part of the pannell George Smith by Mr John Clark [sic] Advocate and lastly by the Lord Justice Clerk.

Betwixt the hours of five and six of the morning of Thursday the 28th August The Lord Justice Clerk and Lords Commissioners of Justiciary ordain the Assize instantly to enclose in this place and to return their verdict in the same place at one o'clock this afternoon; continue the diet against the Pannells till that time; ordain the haill* fifteen assizers and all concerned then to attend each under the pains of law, and the Pannells in the meantime to be carried back to prison.

So this takes us no further forward. On the other hand, Roughead accepted it as it stood and that must weigh heavily indeed in our determination of the 'credibility', even though Mackenzie's 'pretty accurately we think' is less than completely reassuring. Mackenzie's version accords with Clerk's well-known quickness of repartee. 'There's John Clerk, the lame lawyer,' once he overheard a lady say. 'Mem,' he turned on her, 'ah'm a lame man, but ah'm no a lame lawyer.' It is in keeping with what we know of his drinking habits. With Charles Hay (Lord Newton) and Lord Hermand he was to belong to the last generation of really formidable

* Note the Scottish accent coming through.

judicial topers in Edinburgh. Clerk was on his feet for a whole hour; *something* happened during that space of time which Creech felt it necessary to suppress and Morison to abridge. Lastly what Morison retained of the hurly-burly in his printed *Trial* tends to confirm Mackenzie (who, though working on Morison's notes, does not seem to have had his printed *Trial* by him). In particular the words Morison put in Clerk's mouth in the *Trial* ('I have been snubbed rather too often my Lord') point to a good deal more altercation having taken place than he reported.

Brodie of Brodie's petition to the Home Secretary is to be found in Home Office: Scotland, Criminal Papers HO 102 Vol. 51 (copies of which are in the Scottish Record Office).

The Deacon's Will is written in a copy of Aeneas Morison's narrative of the trial in the National Library of Scotland. This copy was presented to the Library in 1919 by Lord Guthrie, a distinguished Scots judge of his day (and, as it happens, an Old College acquaintance of R.L.S.).

Regrettably, nothing of the Brodie case survives in the records of the Crown Office, Edinburgh. I am grateful to the Crown Agent for confirming that this is so.

Appendix I

The Case of George White, as reported in the Books of Adjournal of the High Court of Justiciary, 4 August 1788

George White 'tanner in Pleasance in Edinburgh, present prisoner in the Tolbooth of Edinburgh' was indicted before Lords Braxfield, Henderland, Rae, Stonefield and Swinton for murder or alternatively culpable homicide

in so far as on the night of the twentieth day of the month of November 1787 . . . you the said George White having gone into the house of James McArthur, late smith and changekeeper in Halkerston's Wynd in Edinburgh and a quarrel having there arose and a scuffle ensued betwixt you and the said James McArthur you thereafter left the said house and did afterwards on the same night return to that house alongst with William Peacock butcher in Edinburgh and John Brown residenter there; and having gone into the house you the said George White did then and there violently assault the said James McArthur and did strike him a violent blow on the head with a bottle by which blows his head was cut and wounded, and the said James McArthur, having been thrown into a fever in consequence of these wounds did die in a few weeks thereafter, the death of the said James McArthur being occasioned by the blows given him. . . .

White pleaded not guilty. Mr John Pattison, the advocate appearing for the prisoner with Mr William Honeyman, and Mr George Fergusson (later the famous Lord Hermand), represented that the indictment indicated no felonious intent, that there had only been 'a scuffle', and that it did not say who was the aggressor, and 'that the bottle and the candlestick were not brought by the Pannell, they were in the house and might have been used against him. . . .'

The indictment was found relevant and a jury was picked (including Mr Alexander Bruce of the shop on the North

Bridge) and witnesses were produced to establish the prosecution's case, which was conducted by the Solicitor-General.
One of these witnesses was McArthur's widow.

To this witness it was objectioned on the part of the Pannell that
she is of infamous character and as such intestible. That she and her
husband not only for years past kept an infamous house of bad fame
in the city of Edinburgh but that as far back as 1775 they were tried
and banished from the village and Barony of Gorbals of Glasgow by
the Bailies of that jurisdiction for keeping a common stew and
disturbing and breaking the public peace before coming to this
place. . . .

This objection against Mistress McArthur's admissibility
was repelled. Other witnesses for the Prosecution were Mr Tapp
the goldsmith of Parliament Square (was he, one wonders,
another of the house's clientele?) and the surgeon and drug-
gist who attended to Mr McArthur's cracked skull.

The defence witnesses were then produced including 'John
Paterson, one of the City Guard' but there is, of course, no
indication of their testimony just as it is not possible to say how
hard the Crown pressed its case. Dundas summed up for the
Prosecution, Fergusson for the Defence. It may by now have
been late into the night, for Braxfield ordained the jury to
return their verdict by half past one the following day.

By a majority White was found guilty of culpable homicide.
Surprisingly, Braxfield deferred the sentencing until the following day. (As it happened the immediately succeeding business
both on this day and the previous one was formally to continue
the diet against Brodie and Smith.)

On 7 August Braxfield intimated the sentence: a mere eight
months' imprisonment in the Tolbooth and a fine of 500 marks
Scots (a modest sum indeed) 'to be paid in to the Treasurer of
the Orphan Hospital of Edinburgh'. White also was bound
over to keep the peace for two years under penalty of a fine.

What is to read into this it is hard to say. But it is a possible
inference that Brown the Irish 'heavy' was recognized to have
been more than a spectator. And it was in these days of August
that the Crown authorities had much in mind the crucial part
Brown must play in the presentation of their case against the
Deacon – as is suggested by their postponements of the trial
date which was originally intended to be mid-August.

Reporting the trial of George White the errant Inspector of Hides, the *Edinburgh Magazine* for August 1788 reports the facts of the case – the bottle, the candlestick and McArthur's smashed head. Then it reports that he was found guilty of *culpable homicide* (the italics the *Edinburgh Magazine*'s, not mine).

Appendix II

John Clerk's Bellicosity
Excerpt from Lord Cockburn's Journal

13th February 1848. I have just seen the following passage in the last number of the *Quarterly Review* (No. 163, art. 2, p. 76): 'We may add that even within the last twenty-five years, at a sitting of the Second Division of the Court of Session, such words passed between one of the Judges on the Bench, Lord Glenlee, and the celebrated John Clerk (afterwards Lord Eldin), at the Bar, that the Court was instantly called on by the Lord-Advocate Maconochie (since Lord Meadowbank), to take such measures as would prevent a dual between these highly reverend sexagenarians; two certainly of the most accomplished gentlemen, as well as lawyers, of their time.' Since this strange scene has got into print it may be as well to tell it correctly. I was present and witnessed it.

All that is said about Maconochie is erroneous. I believe he was not Lord-Advocate, but on the Bench at the time; at any rate, he most certainly was not present. Nor was there any interference by any Lord-Advocate. I don't recollect, and can't ascertain, the exact date of the occurrence; but I am pretty confident that it must have been some time between November 1819 and November 1823.

The Judges present were Boyle (the Justice-Clerk), and Lords Robertson, Bannatyne, and Craigie. After the usual wrangle at the Bar, the Court began to decide a commonplace cause. Glenlee, then about three score and ten, had just commenced, when Clerk, who was counsel for one of the parties, rose, plainly to say something more, but in a way perfectly inoffensive, and though irregular not very unusual. Glenlee, contrary to his usual patience and good-breeding, instantly said – 'Na, Mr Clerk. I'm not to be interrupted. That's really impertinent.' Clerk was in a blaze in a moment.

'Impertinent! I wish you would say that anywhere else.'
Glenlee, famous once at the small sword, and a thorough
gentleman, instead of shrinking behind his gown, fired up too,
and answered – 'I'll say it wherever you like!!' The bar, and
the audience and the bench were dumbfounded. At last the
head of the Court (Boyle) broke in, and declared that a gross
impropriety had been committed, and that nothing could be
done till Mr Clerk made an ample apology. Poor worthy Lord
Craigie, ever afraid of mischief, looked exactly as I suppose his
uncle the Lord President did in 1757, at the outbreak between
Wedderburn and Lockhart, when he 'felt his flesh creep on
his bones'. Bannatyne, the Celt, was one of the unfortunate
wretches who cannot keep their beds in the morning, and, as
usual, early rising made him sleep most of the day. He stared,
just awakened, and smiled, and seemed to wonder what it was
all about. Robertson, who was deaf, unfortunately asked what
had happened, which obliged Boyle to repeat it all, loudly, into
his trumpet, a recital which made it all look heavier and more
serious than it was.

Most people off the bench thought the apology ought rather
to have been required from Glenlee. However, since it was
imperatively ordered to be made by Clerk, I trembled for the
result, for I expected him to repeat the defiance. But the
instinct that never failed to come to his aid in every professional
peril, saved him. He kept his own, and gave the lord worse
than he had yet got. 'My Lord,' said he, in a calm, firm,
resolute style, 'I'll make no apology!' This produced another
united order from all the Judges. 'Very well, my Lords,' said
Clerk, with a soft sly sneer, 'since your Lordships will have it,
I'll make an apology! But it shall be an apology to the Court.
For I'll make no apology to my Lord Glenlee!' (these last
words with contemptuous birr). This made bad worse; and
there was a more positive order for an instant apology 'to Lord
Glenlee'. Then came the triumph of Clerk's skill. Drawing
himself up, full length, on his sound leg, and surveying them
all, as a terrier does a rat that he means to worry at a bite,
calmly and scornfully, and with a half-smiling leer at what he
knew he was going to do, he said, steadily and coolly, 'Very
well, my Lords, since your Lordships insist upon't, I now make
an apology to Lord Glenlee, IN RESPECT OF YOUR LORD-
SHIPS' COMMANDS!!' These last words were spoken with the

utmost scorn – as much as to say, what the better are ye of that, my Lord? And everybody felt that the insult was repeated; but the Court was thankful to get out of the affair on any decent pretext, and I felt relieved when the scene was over. Glenlee said nothing; which was thought shabby.

Bibliography

The trial

High Court of Justiciary Records, Scottish Record Office, Edinburgh.

CREECH, William. *An Account of the Trial of William Brodie and George Smith,* Printed for William Creech, 1788.

MACKENZIE, Peter. *Reminiscences of Glasgow and the West of Scotland,* vol. 2, Glasgow 1866.

MORISON, Aeneas. *The Trial of William Brodie, Wright and Cabinet-maker in Edinburgh, and of George Smith, Grocer there, before the High Court of Justiciary,* Edinburgh, 1788.

ROUGHEAD, William, W.S. *The Trial of Deacon Brodie,* 1906 (Notable Scottish Trials series).

The Edinburgh Evening Courant.

The Edinburgh Magazine.

Biographical and topographical works

ADAM, Sir Charles E., ed. *The Political State of Scotland in the Last Century: a confidential report on the political opinions, family connections or personal connections of the 2662 county voters in 1788.* 1887.

ALLARDYCE, A., ed. *Scotland and Scotsmen of the Eighteenth Century* (John Ramsay of Ochtertyre), 2 vols, 1888 [for descriptions of the judges].

ARNOT, Hugo. *History of Edinburgh,* Edinburgh, 1779.

BOSWELL, James. *The Private Papers of James Boswell,* Yale edition: [particularly *Boswell for the Defense,* McGraw–Hill, 1959].

CHAMBERS, Robert. *Traditions of Edinburgh,* 1825.

CHAMBERS, William, and CHAMBERS, Robert. *Minor Antiquities of Edinburgh,* 1833.

CLARK, A. Melville. *Sir Walter Scott, the Formative Years*, Blackwood, 1971.

COCKBURN, Henry. *Memorials of His Time*, Edinburgh, 1856.

CREECH, William. *Edinburgh Fugitive Pieces with Letters*, 1815.

FERGUSON, William. *Scotland 1689 to the Present*, Oliver & Boyd, 1968.

FERGUSSON, A. *The Hon. Henry Erskine*, 1882.

KAY, John. *Kay's Portraits: A series of original portraits and caricature etchings by the late John Kay with biographical and illustrative anecdotes*, Edinburgh, 1887.

MCELROY, Davis D. *Scotland's Age of Improvement: a survey of eighteenth-century literary clubs and societies*, Washington State University Press, 1969.

PENNANT, Thomas. *A Tour of Scotland, 1771.*

ROUGHEAD, William, W.S. *The Riddle of the Ruthvens and Other Studies*, Edinburgh, W. Green, 1919 [for an important essay on Lord Braxfield].

SCOTT, Sir Walter. 'A general account of Edinburgh' in his *The Provincial Antiquities and Picturesque Scenery of Scotland*, 1826.

THOMPSON, Harold William, ed. *The Anecdotes and Egotisms of Henry Mackenzie 1745–1831*, Oxford University Press, 1927.

TOPHAM, Edward. *Letters from Edinburgh written in the years 1774, 1775 and 1776.*

A Journey through Part of England and Scotland along with the Army under the Command of H.R.H. the Duke of Cumberland: by a Volunteer, London, 1747.

The Book of the Old Edinburgh Club, vols I–XXXII. [This is by far the most authoritative general source for information about old Edinburgh. For Brodie in particular see vols XXIV, 'Diary of George Sandy', and XXXII, 'Edinburgh furniture and cabinet-makers of the eighteenth century'.]

Robert Louis Stevenson

STEVENSON, R. L. *Edinburgh: Picturesque notes*, 1879.

STEVENSON, R. L. *The Strange Case of Dr Jekyll and Mr Hyde*, Folio Society edition, with an introduction by John Hampden, Folio Society, 1947.

STEVENSON, R. L., and HENLEY, W. E. *Deacon Brodie, or The*

Double Life [1892] in *The Works of Robert Louis Stevenson: Plays*, Heinemann, 1925.

STEVENSON, R. L. *The Collected Poems*, ed. Janet Adam Smith, Hart-Davis, 1950.

R.L.S., Stevenson's Letters to Charles Baxter ed. de Lancey Ferguson and Marshall Waingrow; Geoffrey Cumberlege, Oxford University Press, 1956.

CHESTERTON, G. K. *Robert Louis Stevenson*, 2nd edn, Hodder & Stoughton, 1927.

COOPER, Lettice. *Robert Louis Stevenson*, Home & Van Thal, 1947.

DAICHES, David. *Robert Louis Stevenson and His World*, Thames & Hudson, 1973.

FURNAS, J. C. *Voyage to Windward*, Faber, 1952.

MACLAREN, Moray. *Stevenson and Edinburgh*, Chapman & Hall, 1950.

POPE-HENNESSY, J. *Robert Louis Stevenson*, Cape, 1974.

SIMPSON, E. Blantyre. *Robert Louis Stevenson's Edinburgh Days*, 1898.

STEUART, J. E. *Robert Louis Stevenson*, 2 vols, Sampson Low, Marston, 1924.

A STEVENSON LIBRARY: Catalogue of a collection of writings by and about Robert Louis Stevenson, formed by E. J. Beinecke; Vol. 4, Letters to and about Robert Louis Stevenson, Yale University Library, 1958.

Index